For LUCA!

You can draw military aircraft

By Mike Artell

Printed in the United States of America

ISBN 978-0-9910894-4-4

Published by
MJA Creative, LLC
Box 3997
Covington, LA 70434
www.mikeartell.com

For questions, comments, permissions or to book Mike Artell for a personal appearance please email mike@mikeartell.com .

Photo and illustration credits

With the exception of step-by-step drawings and unless otherwise noted, all photos and 3-axis drawings are used courtesy Wikimedia Commons license.

A-10 Thunderbolt – Wikimedia Commons by Daniel J. McLain (Mate 2nd Class),
A-10 Thunderbolt drawing – Wikimedia Commons. Source: https://airdefense.bliss.army.mil
AH-64 Helicopter Wikimedia Commons by Tim Felce (Airwolfhound) (AH-64D Apache Longbow - RIAT 2014) [C BY-SA 2.0 (http://creativecommons.org/licenses/by-sa/2.0)]
AH-64 drawings – Wikimedia Commons by Los688 (Own work)
AV-8 Harrier - Wikimedia Commons - U.S. Navy photo by Mass Communication Specialist 1st Class Grant P. Ammon
AV-8 drawing - http://www.history.navy.mil/museums/paxmuseum/photos/av8b/0401.gif
B1-B Wikimedia Commons by Mstr Sgt. William Greer (https://www.dvidshub.net/image/392024)
B-1B drawing – Wikimedia Commons by Tech. Sgt. Michael Haggerty
B-2 Spirit – Wikimedia Commons, U.S. Air Force, uploaded by Louis Waweru

B-2 Spirit drawing – Wikimedia Commons by NORTHROP_B-2.png: Stahlkocher derivative work: M0tty (NORTHROP_B-2.png)
C-130 photo - Wikimedia Commons, source: Senior Airman Jorge A. Rodriguez, U.S. Air Force.
C-130 drawing - Wikimedia Commons, source: http://c130.robins.af.mil/
CH-47 Wikimedia Commons by DoD photo by Spc. Russell J. Good
CH-47 Chinook drawing - Wikimedia Commons, BOEING VERTOL CH-47 CHINOOK von https://airdefense.bliss.army.mil
F-14 Tomcat - Wikimedia Commons by Navy Camera Operator: PHAA NATHAN LAIRD, USN (ID:DNSD0607288 / 051230N7241L006)
F-14 Tomcat drawing - Wikimedia Commons, https://airdefense.bliss.army.mil
F-16 photo courtesy U.S. Air Force photo/Staff Sgt. David Salanitri, 150408-F-TM170-562.JPG
F-16 drawing - Wikimedia Commons, Source: https://airdefense.bliss.army.mil
F-18 Super Hornet photo - Wikimedia Commons, http://www.defenselink.mil/multimedia/, LCPL JOHN MCGARITY, USMC
F-18 drawing courtesy of NASA Dryden Flight Research Center
F-22 Wikimedia Commons by Rob Shenk from Great Falls, VA, USA (F-22 Raptor Uploaded by Diaa abdelmoneim) [CC BY-SA 2.0]
F-22 drawing, Wikimedia Commons by Steal88 (Own work) [GFDL (http://www.gnu.org/copyleft/fdl.html)
F-35 photo - Wikimedia Commons by U.S. Navy – no other attribution
F-35 grayscale drawing - by F-35A_Front.jpg: www.jsf.mil F-35A_Side.jpg: www.jsf.mil
MQ-1B Predator photo - Wikimedia Commons, source: U.S. Air Force. http://www.af.mil/shared/media/photodb/photos/030813-F-8888W-006.jpg
MQ-1B Predator drone drawing - Department of the Air Force, http://www.wbdg.org/ccb/AF/AFETL/etl_09_1.pdf page 16
UH-60 Blackhawk photo –Wikimedia Commons by Staff Sgt. Vernell Hall, U.S. Army
UH-60 Blackhawk drawing – Wikimedia Commons - https://airdefense.bliss.army.mil
V- 22 Osprey photo - Wikimedia Commons by James Haseltine (US Air Force)
V-22 Osprey drawing - Wikimedia Commons by Jetijones (Own work) [CC BY 3.0

What the letters mean

The first aircraft in this book is the A-10 Thunderbolt. The letter, "A" means that the Thunderbolt is an ATTACK aircraft. Its job is to seek out and destroy enemy targets and protect troops on the ground. Any aircraft that has an, "A" in its name has a similar job. Sometimes an aircraft has two letters such as the AH-64 Apache helicopter. In that case, the first letter tells you that it's an ATTACK aircraft and the second letter tells you what kind of aircraft it is. The "H" means it's a HELICOPTER.

Here's what the letters of the other aircraft in this book mean:

If the aircraft has the letter **B** in its name that means it's a bomber. Bombers carry heavy loads of bombs, torpedoes or missiles a long distance.

The letter **C** means the aircraft is a cargo aircraft. The job of these aircraft is to move heavy cargo, passengers or medical patients from one place to another.

The letter **F** is used for fighter aircraft. The job of a fighter is to destroy enemy aircraft or missiles.

H means helicopter. Helicopters take off and land vertically (straight up and down).

M means that the aircraft has more than one kind of job. These aircraft usually have special electronics and they are used to support special missions.

The letter **Q** indicates that the aircraft is radio-controlled and unmanned.

V is the letter used for aircraft that are not helicopters but which can takeoff vertically or in a very short space.

What is that funny square thing?

That funny square thing is a QR code. QR stands for "Quick Response." It's a kind of barcode that was first designed for companies that build automobiles. Today, there are "apps" for most smartphones that make it possible for the phones to read QR codes. Smartphone users can find QR Code apps for their smartphone wherever they download their other apps.

Anyone with a QR code reader on their smartphone can open the app and point the camera of their smartphone at any of the QR codes in this book. The app will take them to a video of the aircraft on that page in action. Some videos show the aircraft taking off or landing, other videos show the aircraft refueling in midflight.

A-10 THUNDERBOLT

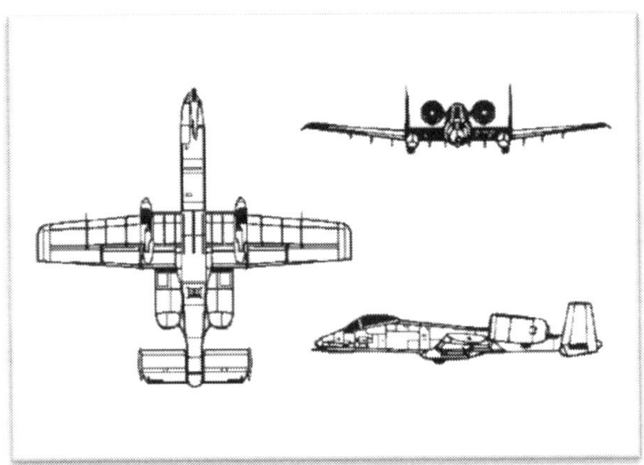

To see video of the A-10 in action, click on the Quick Response (QR) code above or visit https://www.youtube.com/watch?v=7wdPtzm7w1w

The A-10 Thunderbolt is designed to support troops fighting on the ground. Its nickname is, "The Warthog." The A-10 is very tough and can keep flying even if the body of the aircraft is directly hit by large bullets. In fact, it can keep flying with one engine, one tail, and half of one wing missing.

The A-10 is 53 ft. 4 in. (16.26 m) long and 14 ft. 8 in (4.47 m) high. Its wingspan is 57 ft. 6 in (17.53 m) and its top speed is 518 mph (833 km/h).

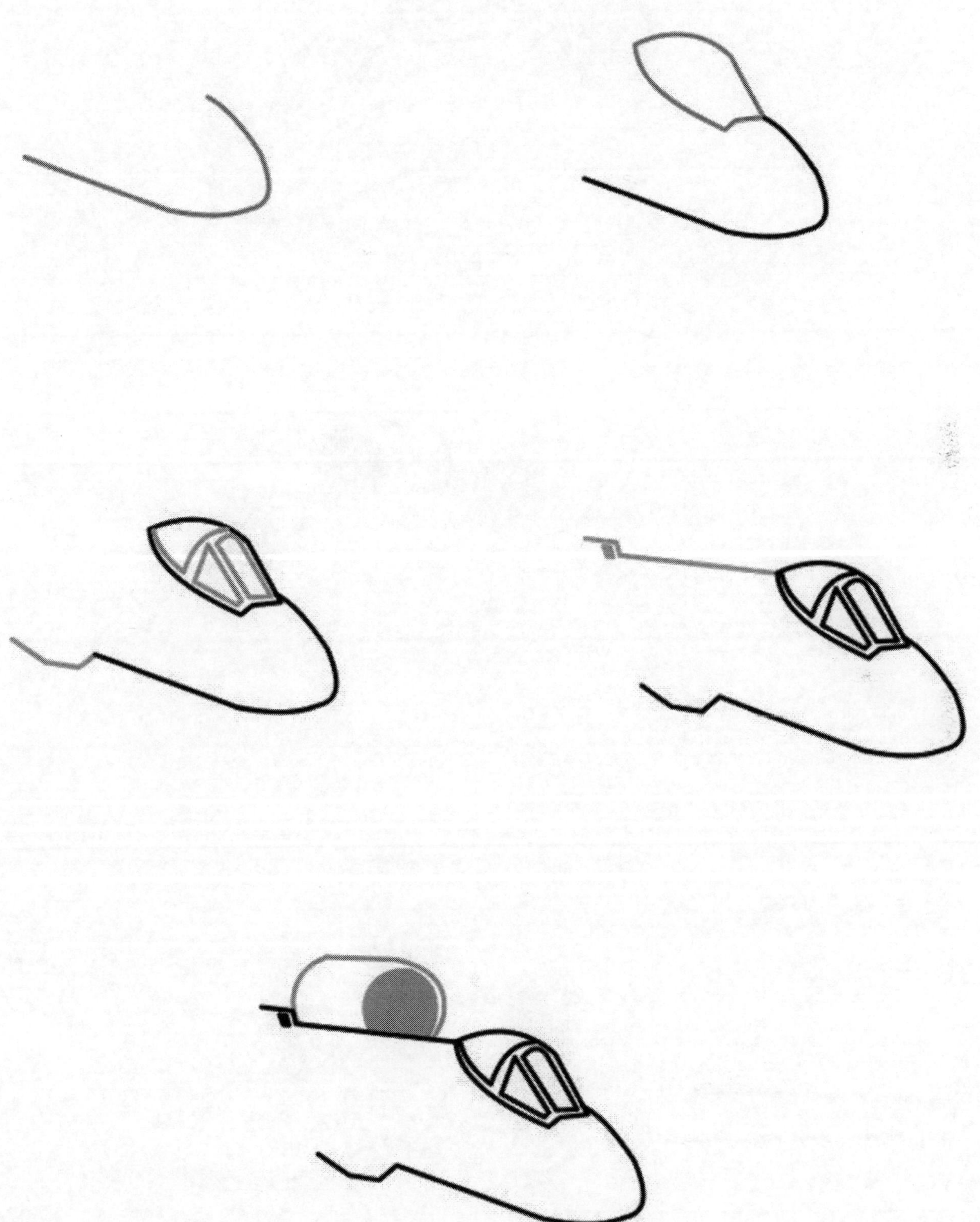

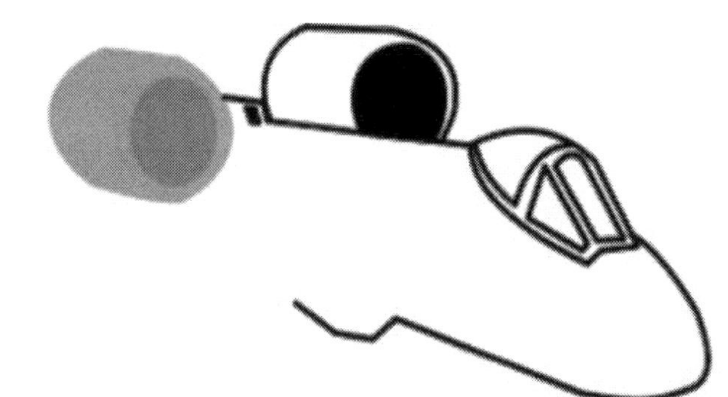

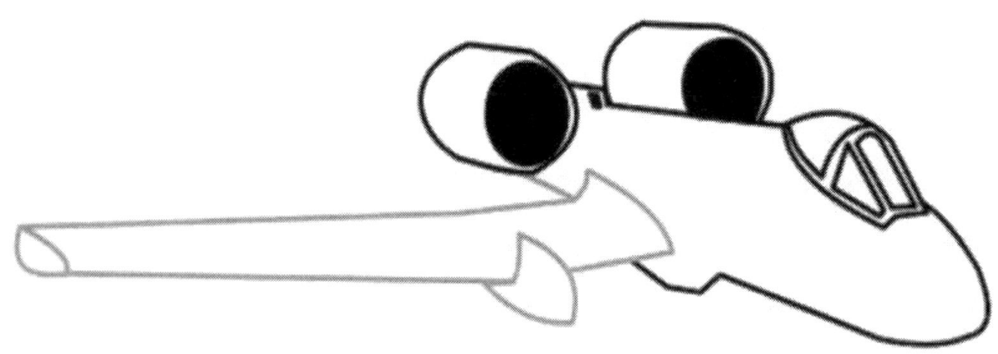

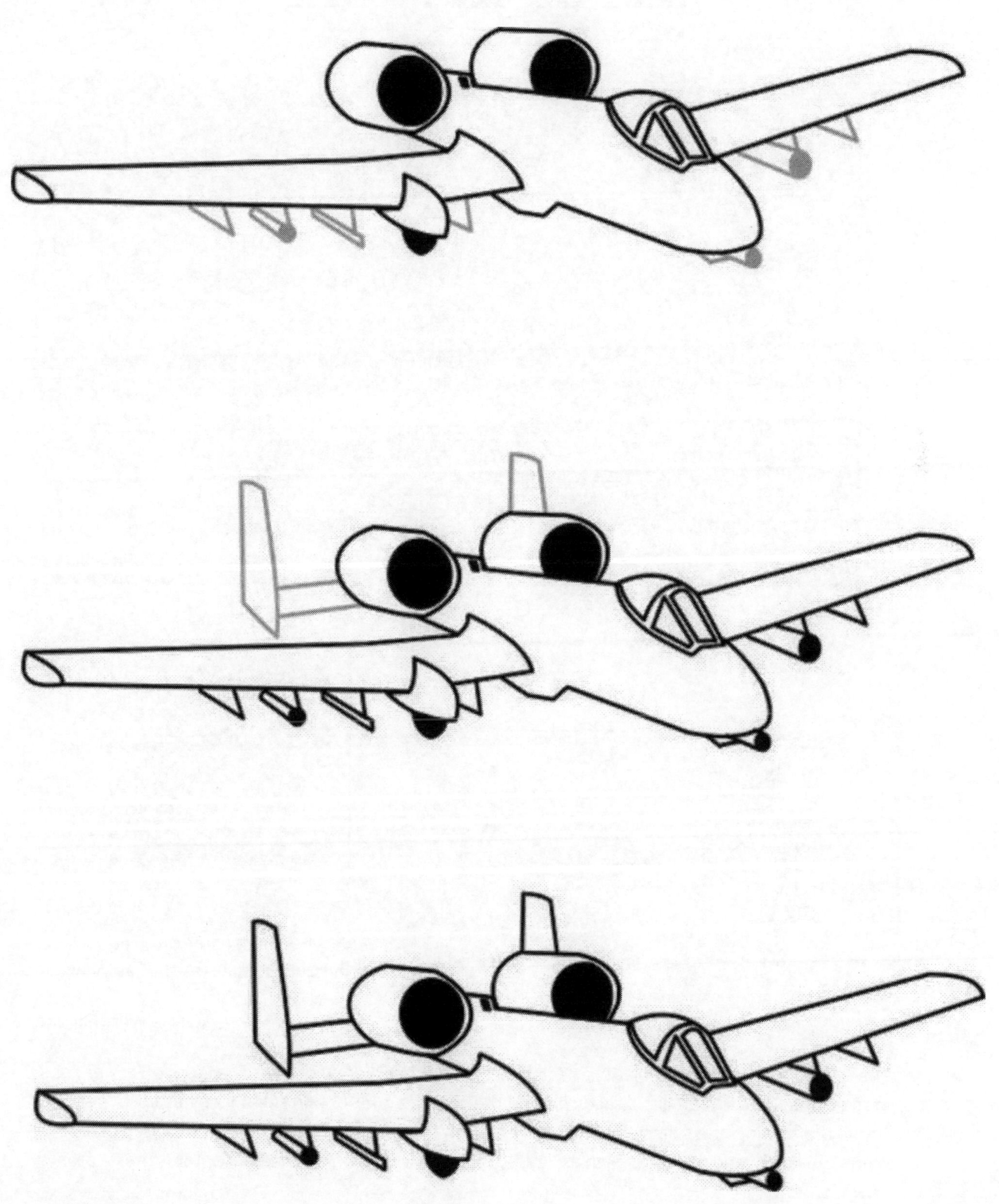

AH-64 APACHE

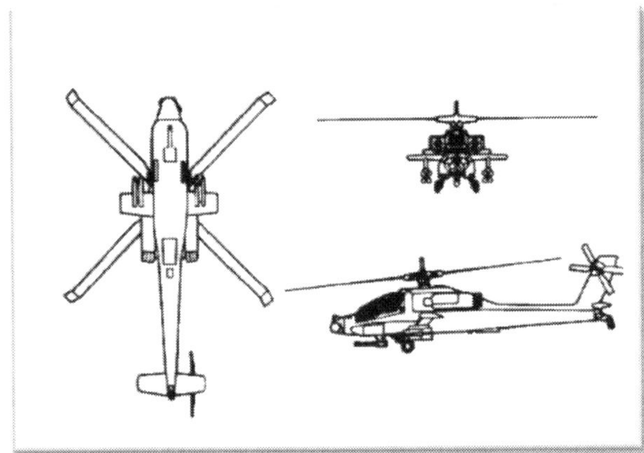

To see video of the AH-64 in action,
click on the Quick Response (QR) code above
or visit
https://www.youtube.com/watch?v=XyEBemkDFeM

The AH-64 Apache is a four-blade, attack helicopter. It has a crew of two. The co-pilot/gunner sits in the front and the pilot sits directly behind the co-pilot/gunner and slightly higher up. When its rotors are turning, the Apache is 58.17 ft. (17.73 m) long. It can reach a maximum speed of 182 mph (293 km/h) and can fly as high as 21,000 ft. (6,400 m). The Apache helicopter is most often flown by Army pilots.

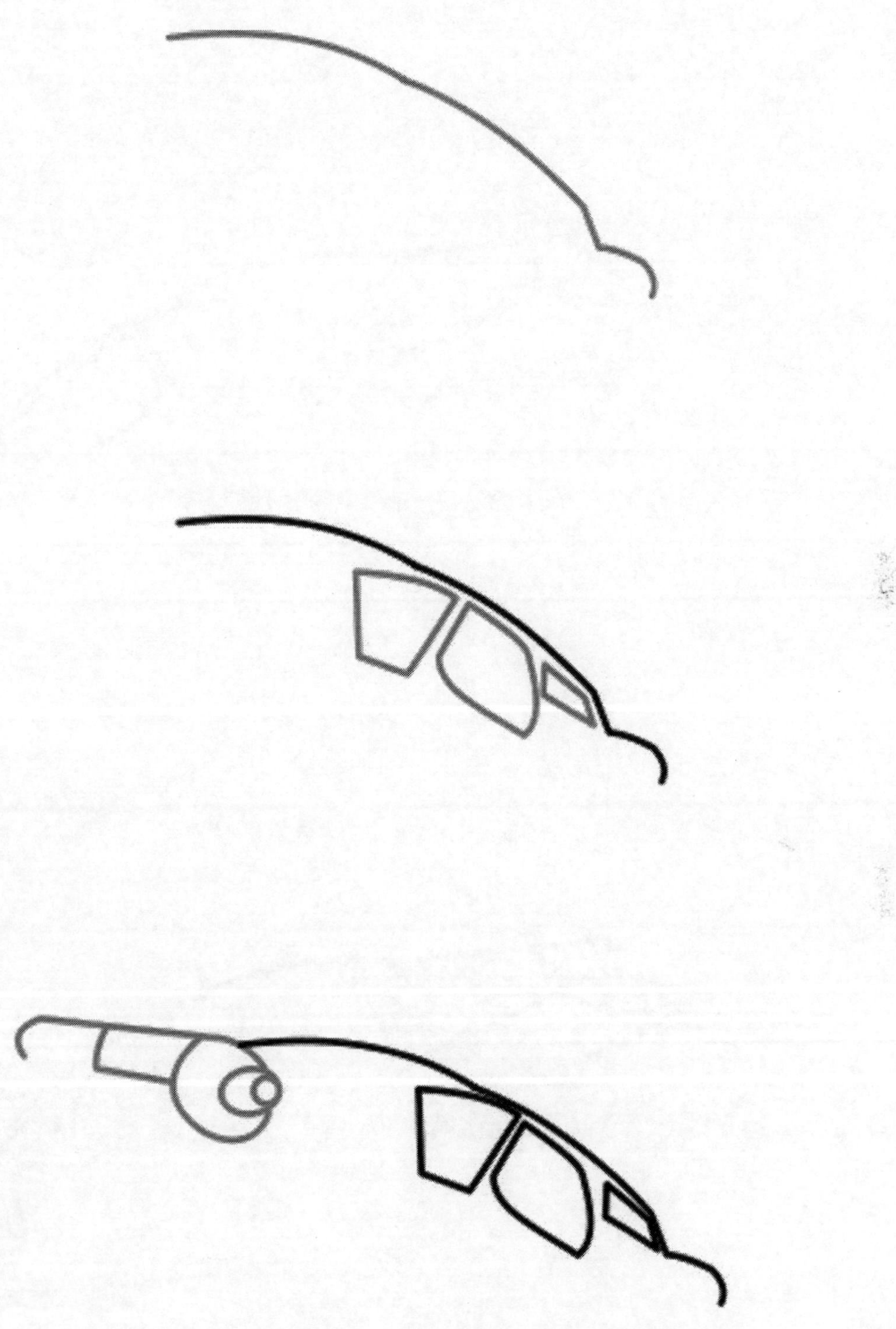

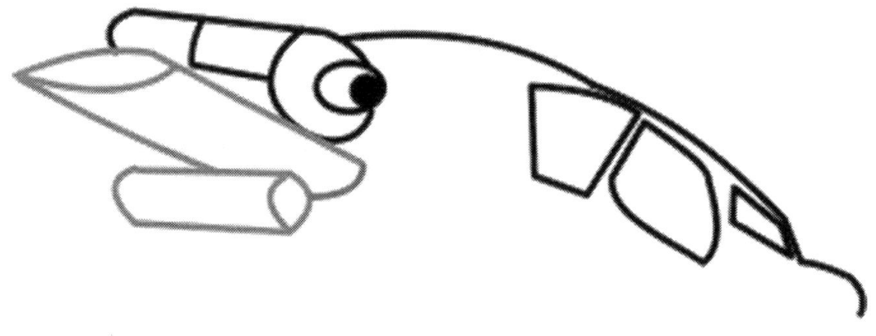

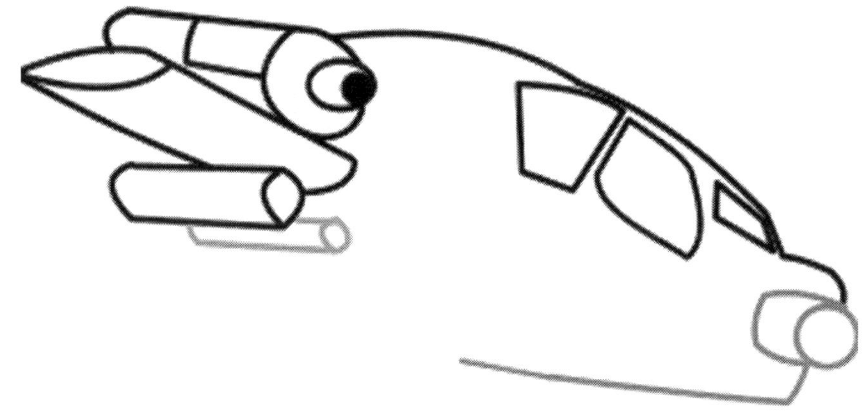

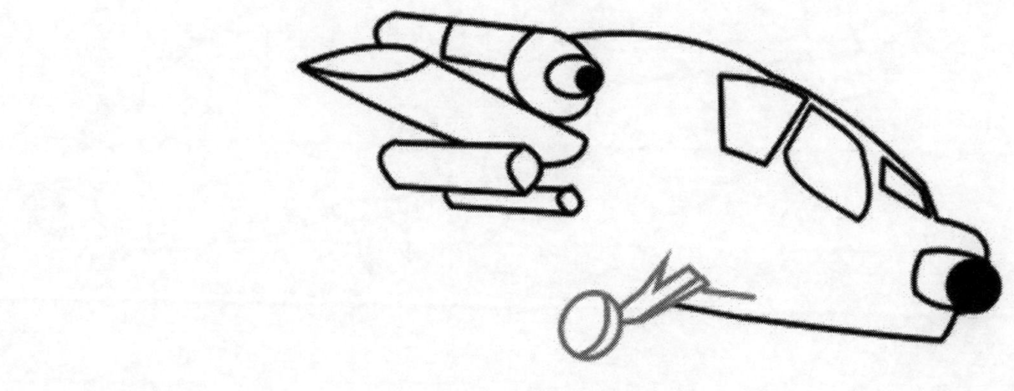

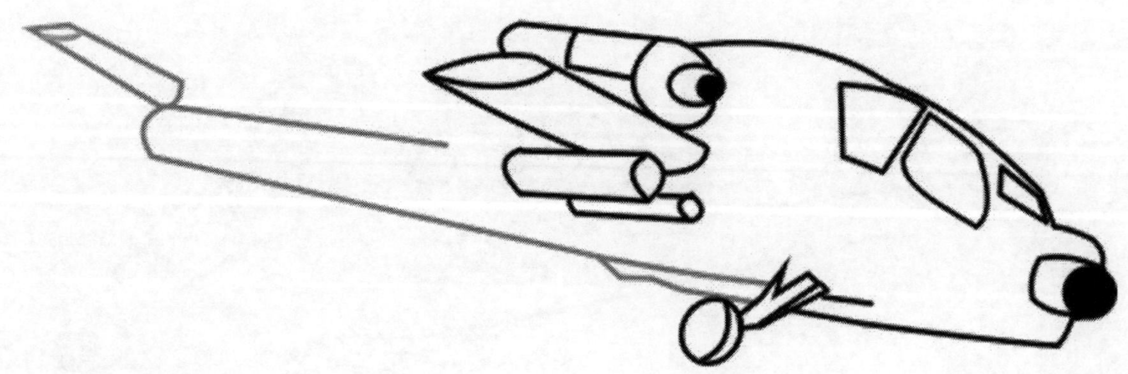

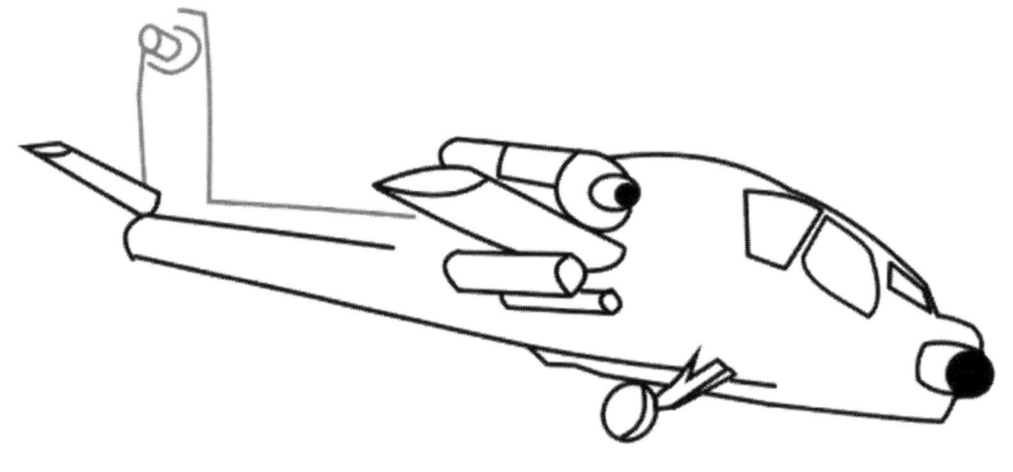

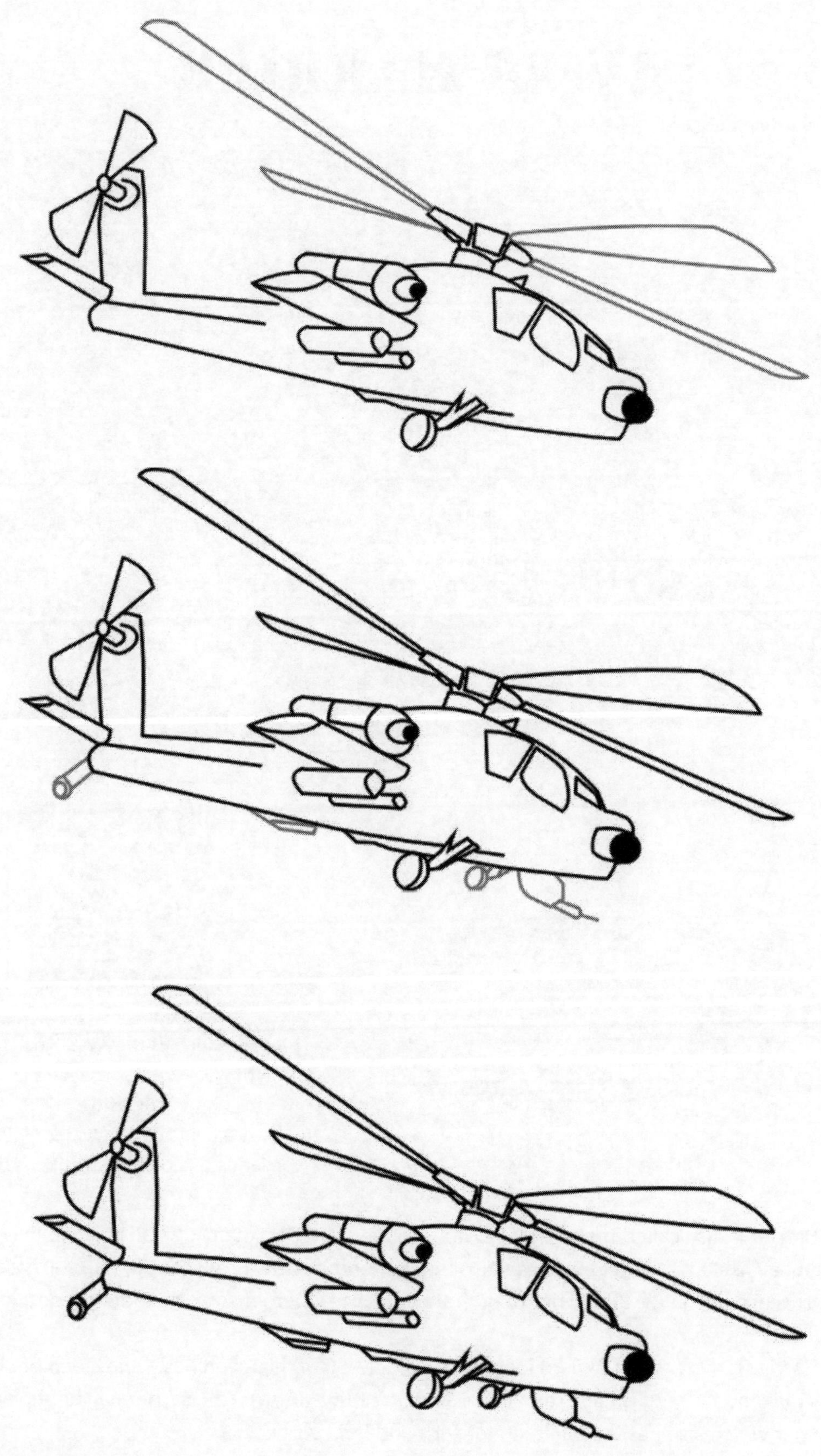

AV-8B HARRIER

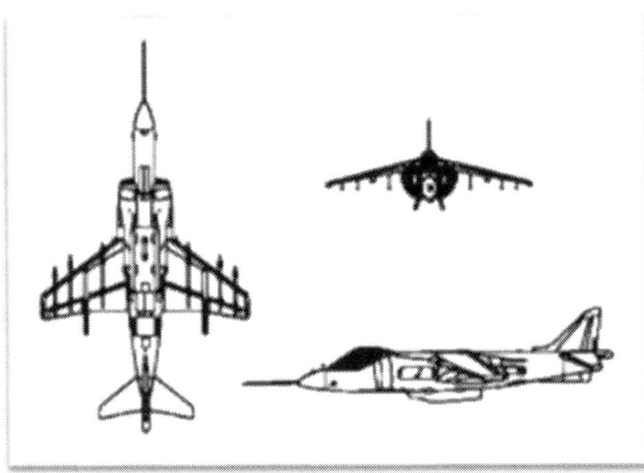

To see video of the AV-8B in action,
click on the Quick Response (QR) code above
or visit
https://www.dvidshub.net/video/84237/av-8b-harrier-iis-takeoff-landing#.VcuY7PlViko

The AV-8B Harrier is also called the Harrier "jump" jet. It got that nickname because it can take off and land on a runway like a typical jet but it can also take off and land vertically (straight up) like a helicopter. This allows the AV-8B Harrier to operate in places where many other jets cannot.

The AV-8B Harrier is 47 ft. 8 in. (14.5 m) long, 11 ft. 8 in. (3.56 m) high and has a wingspan of 30 ft. 4 in. (9.25 m). Its maximum speed is approximately 662 mph (1,065 km/h). The Harrier will be replaced by the F-35 fighter which also has the ability to take off and land vertically.

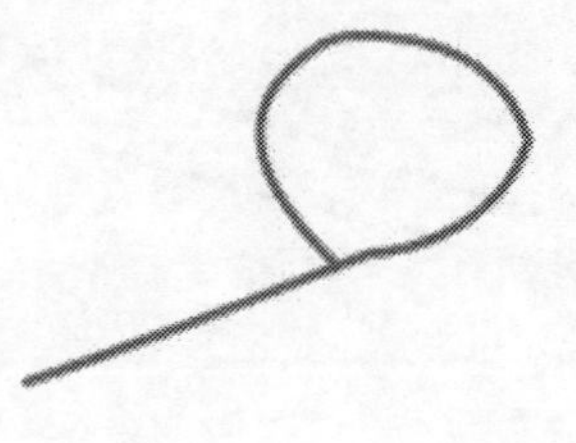

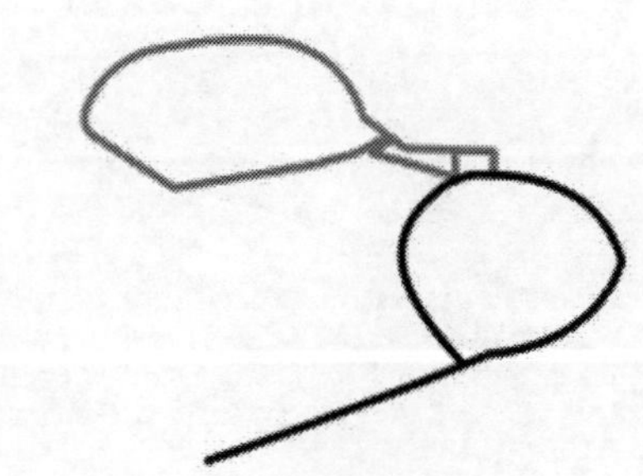

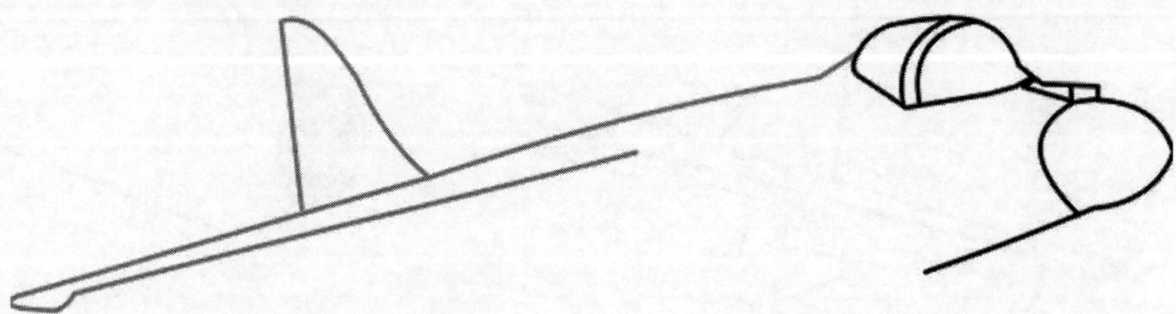

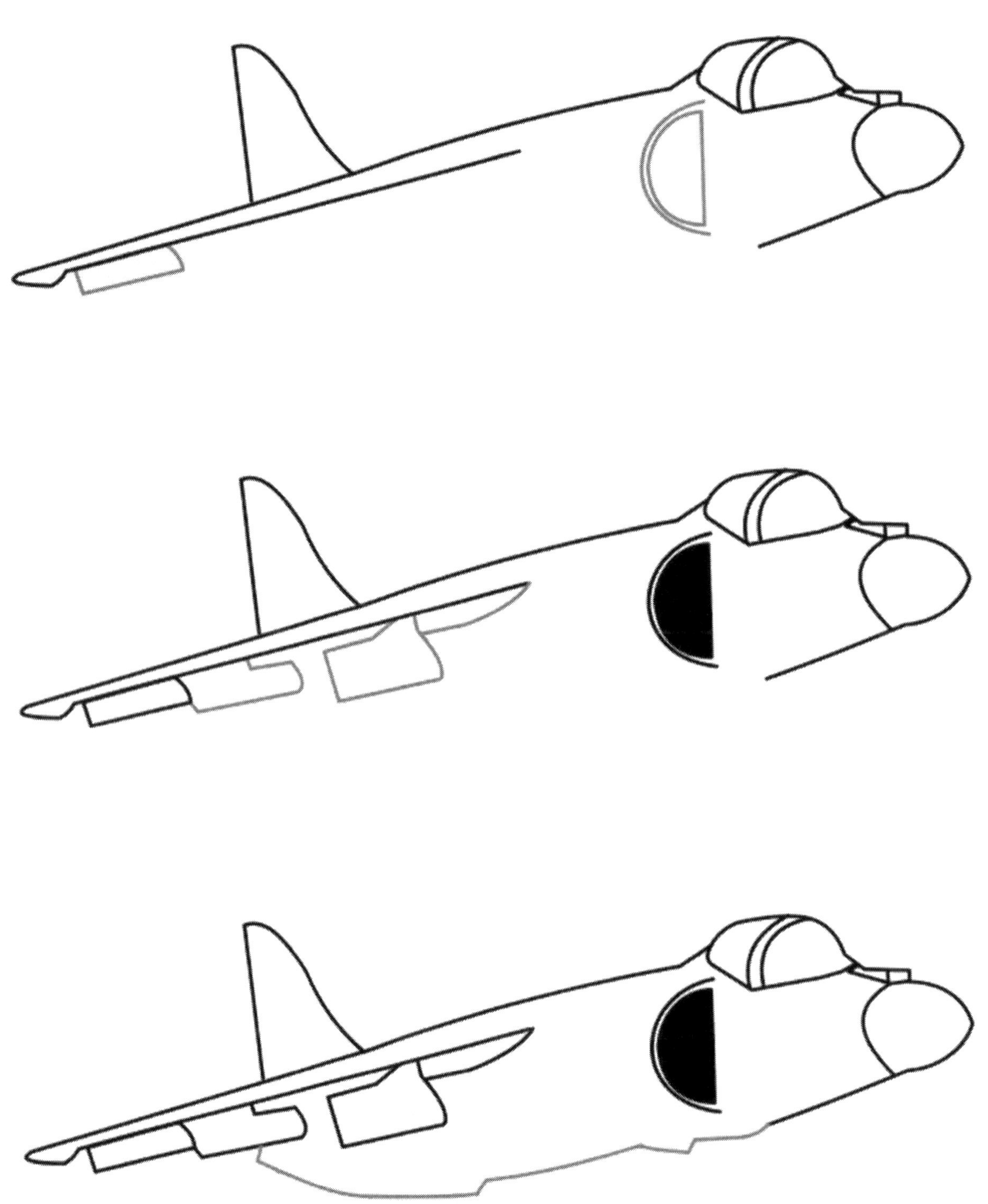

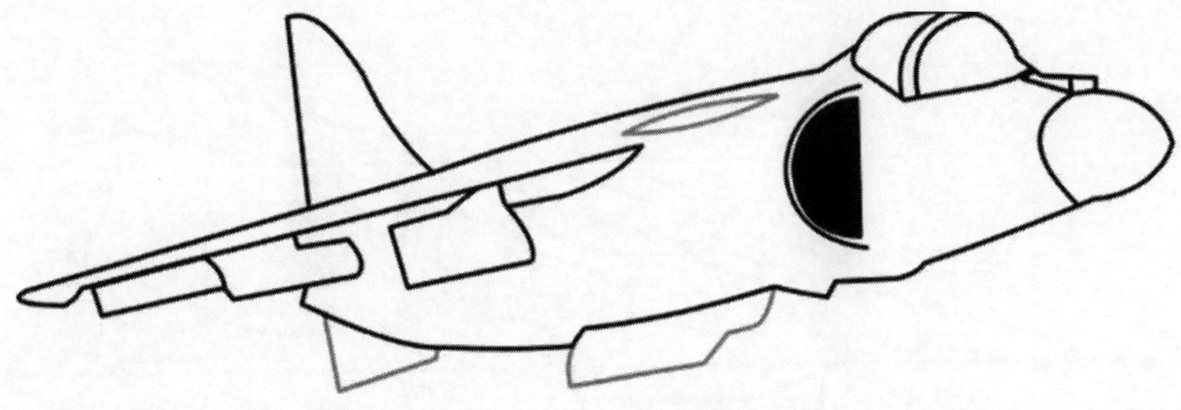

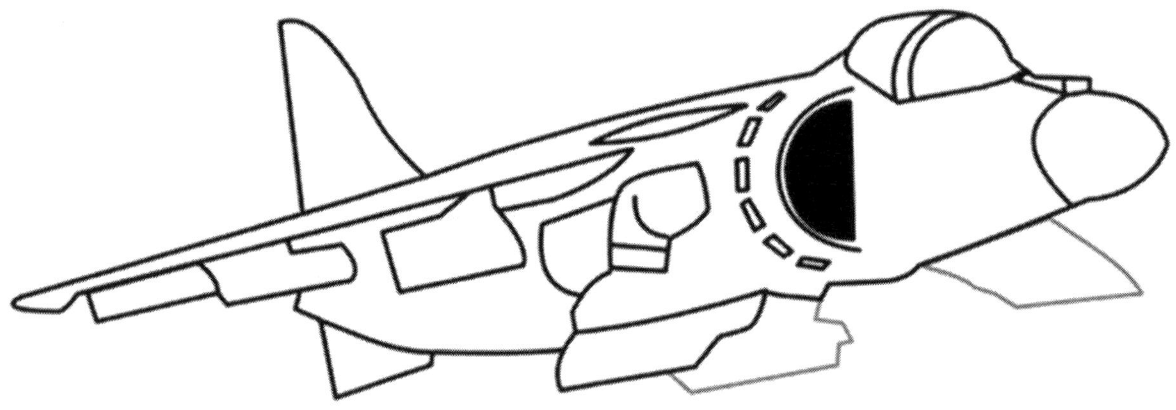

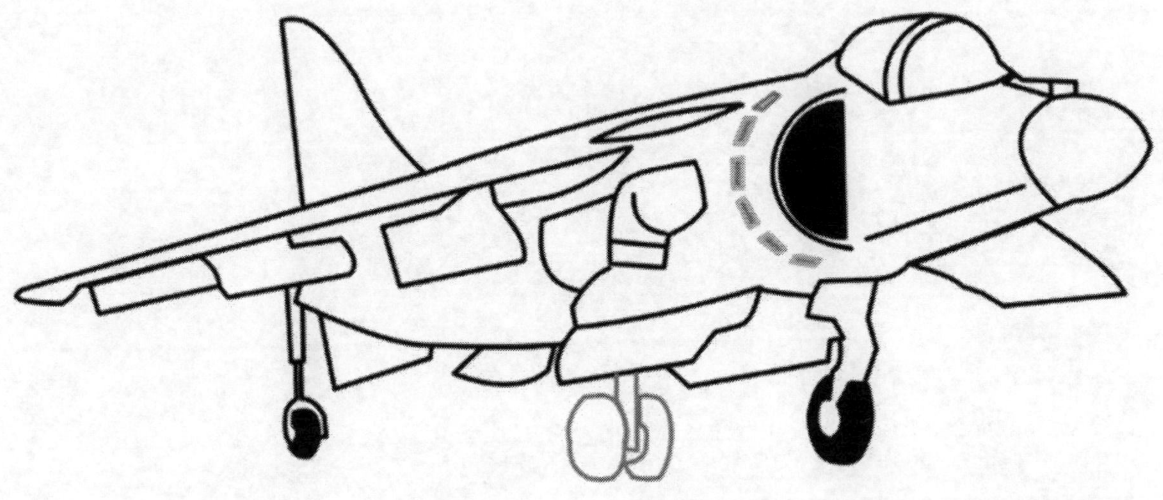

B-1 LANCER

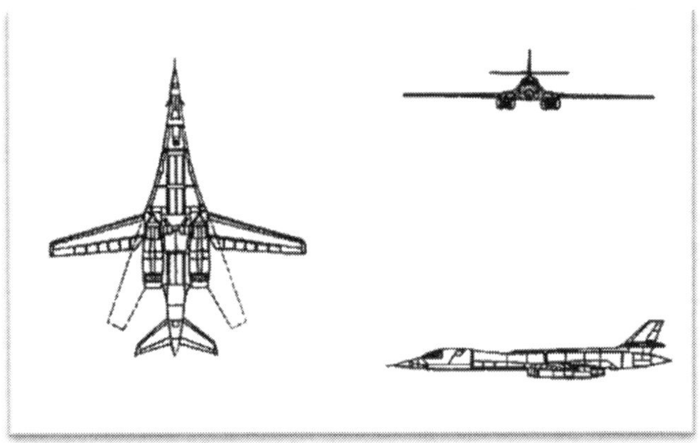

To see video of the B-1 in action,
click on the Quick Response (QR) code above
or visit
https://www.dvidshub.net/video/398839/b-1-mid-air-refueling#.VcOmE_lViko

The B-1 Lancer is 146 ft (44.5 m) long and carries a crew of four. Its wings can be extended out or swept back. When extended, the wingspan is 137 ft (42 m). When swept back, the wingspan is 79 ft (24 m).

At 50,000 ft (15,000 meters) altitude the B-1 can fly at Mach 1.25 (830 mph or 1,335 km/h). At 200–500 ft. (61–152 meters) altitude, the B-1 can fly at Mach 0.92 (700 mph or 1,100 km/h). The B-1 can fly as high as 60,000 ft. (18,000 m).

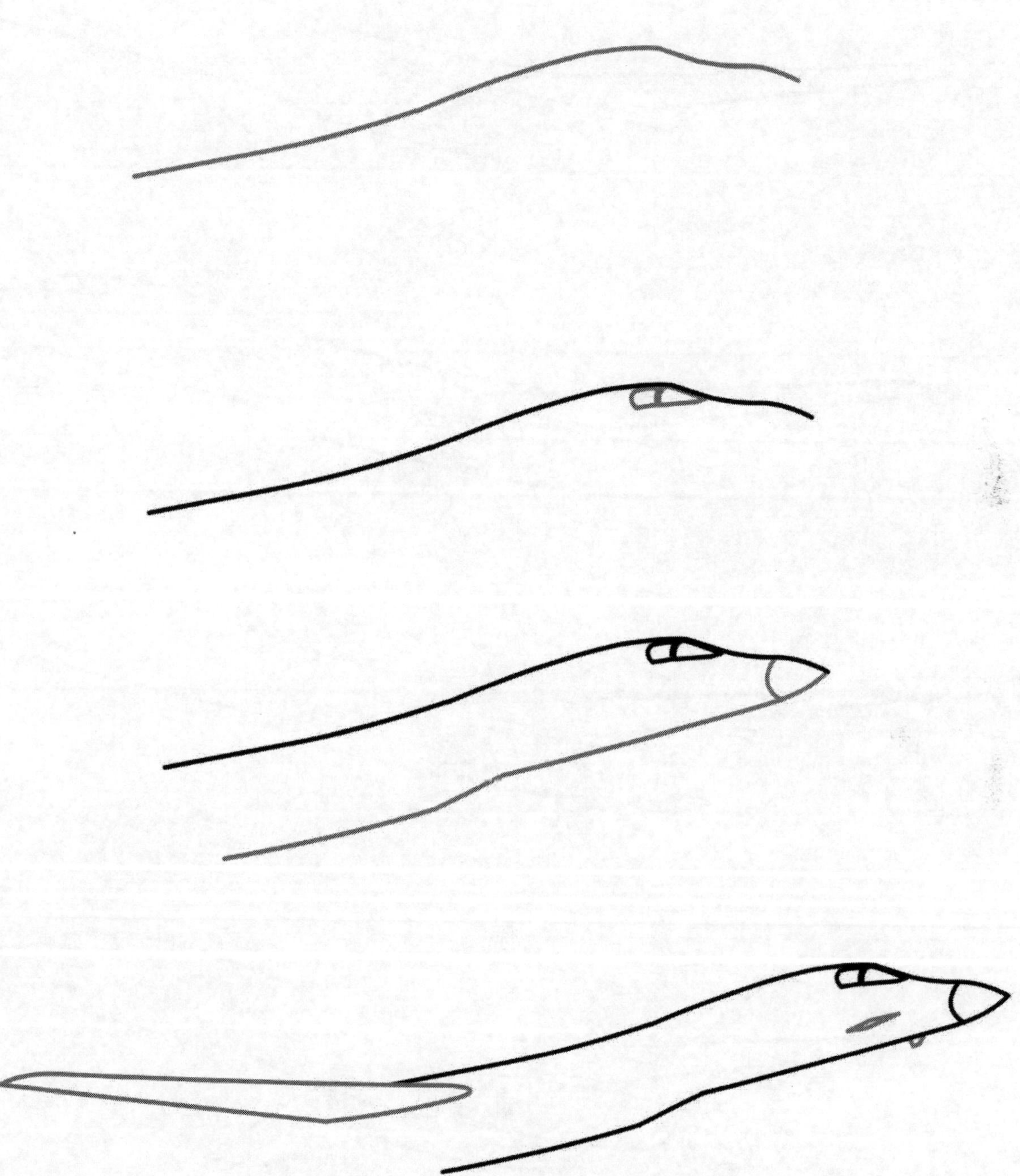

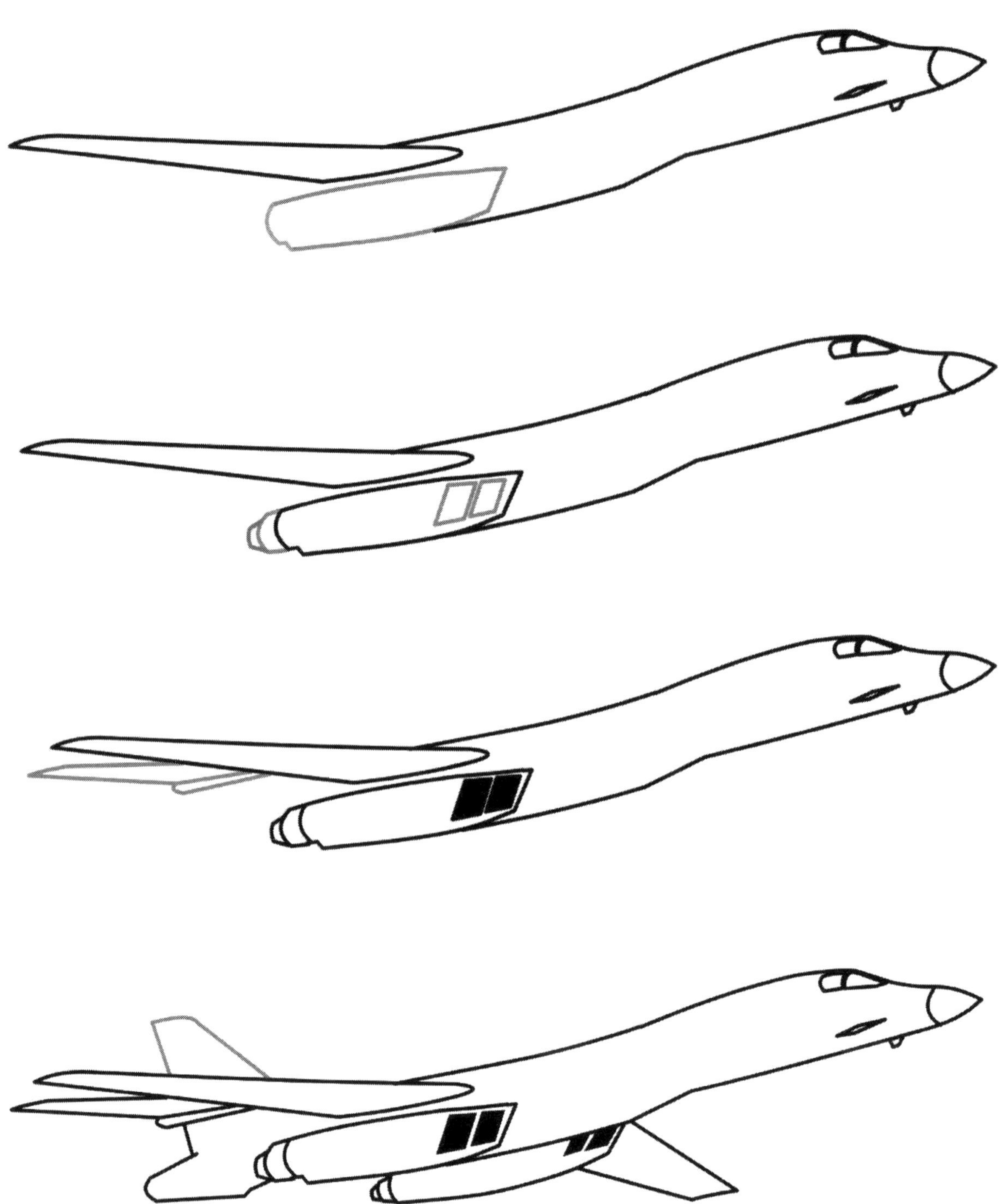

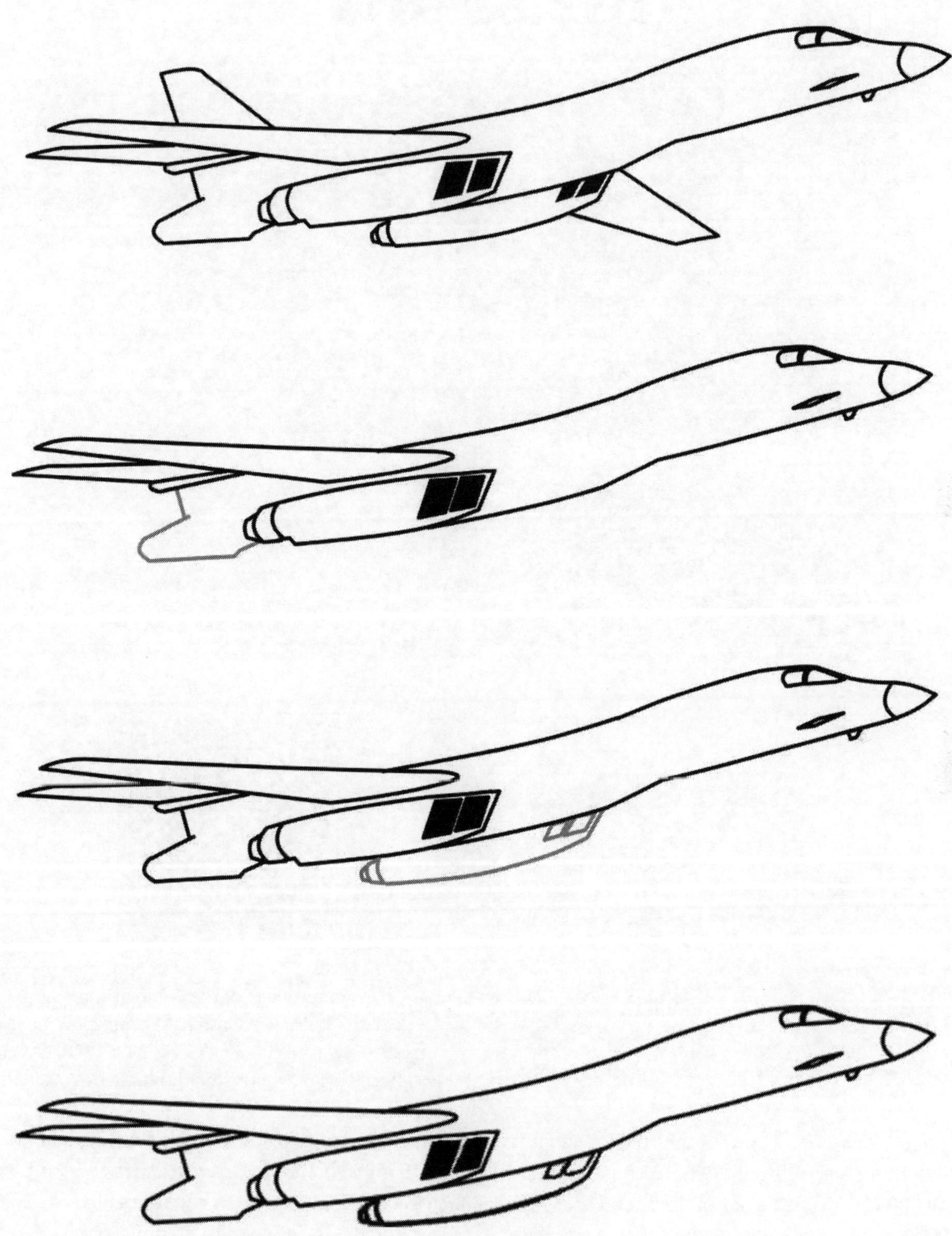

B-2 SPIRIT

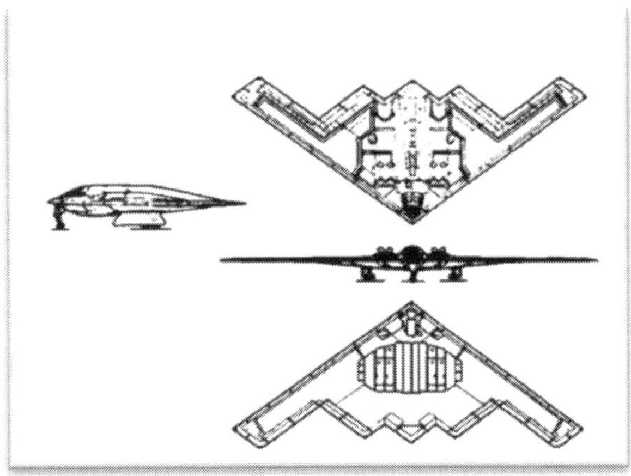

To see video of the B-2 in action,
click on the Quick Response (QR) code above or visit
https://www.dvidshub.net/video/393817/151st-ang-kc-135-refuels-b-2-spirit-stealth-bomber#.VcOxi_lViko

The B-2 Spirit has a crew of two: a pilot and mission commander (co-pilot). The B-2 is shorter than many other bombers. It's only 69 ft. (21.0 m) long and 17 ft. (5.18 m) high. Its wingspan is 172 ft. (52.4 m). At 40,000 ft. altitude its maximum speed is 630 mph (Mach 0.95 or 1,010 km/h). It can fly as high as 50,000 ft. (15,200 m). The B-2 is a "stealth" aircraft. This means that the B-2 is designed to be difficult for enemy defense systems to know where it is and to defend against it.

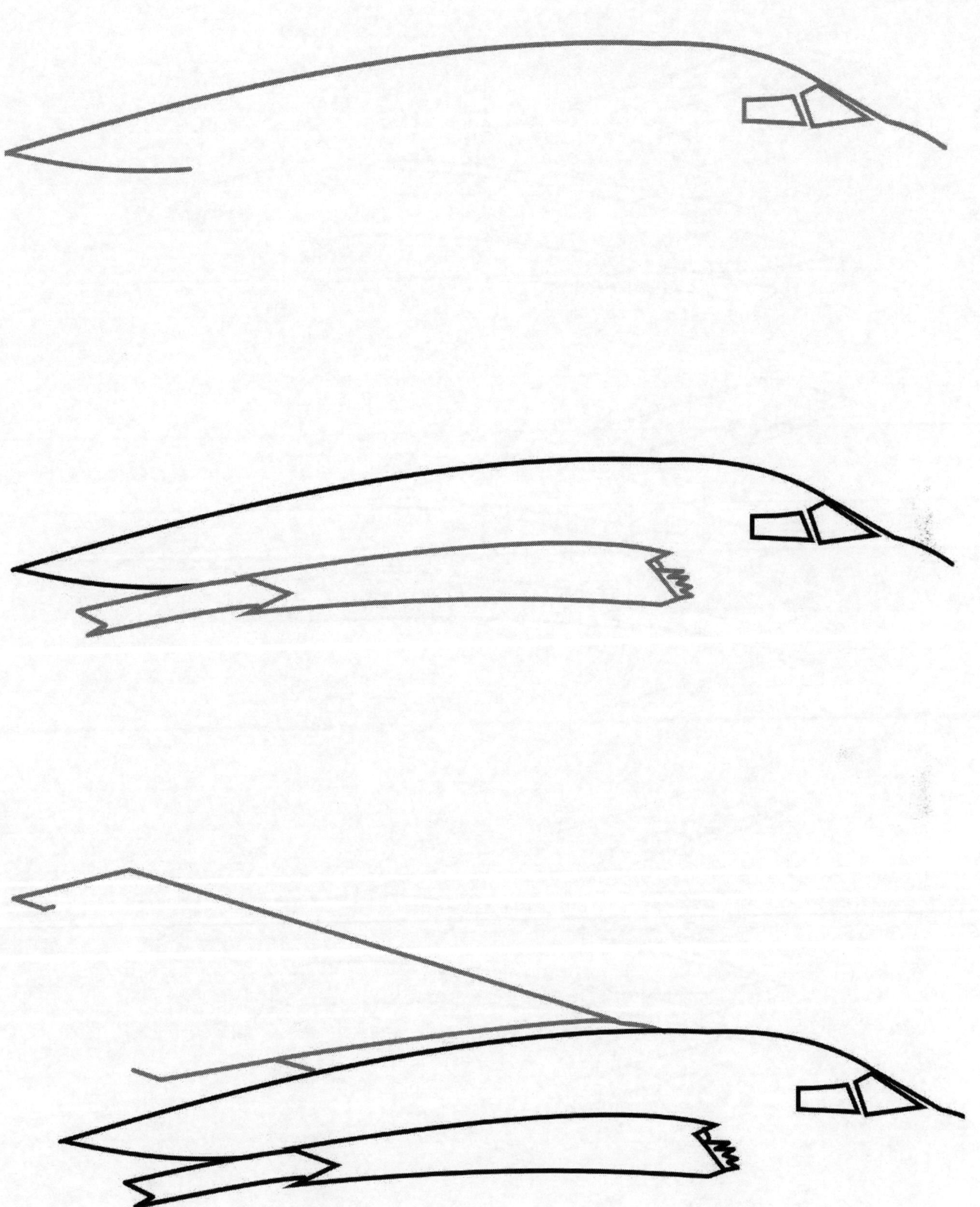

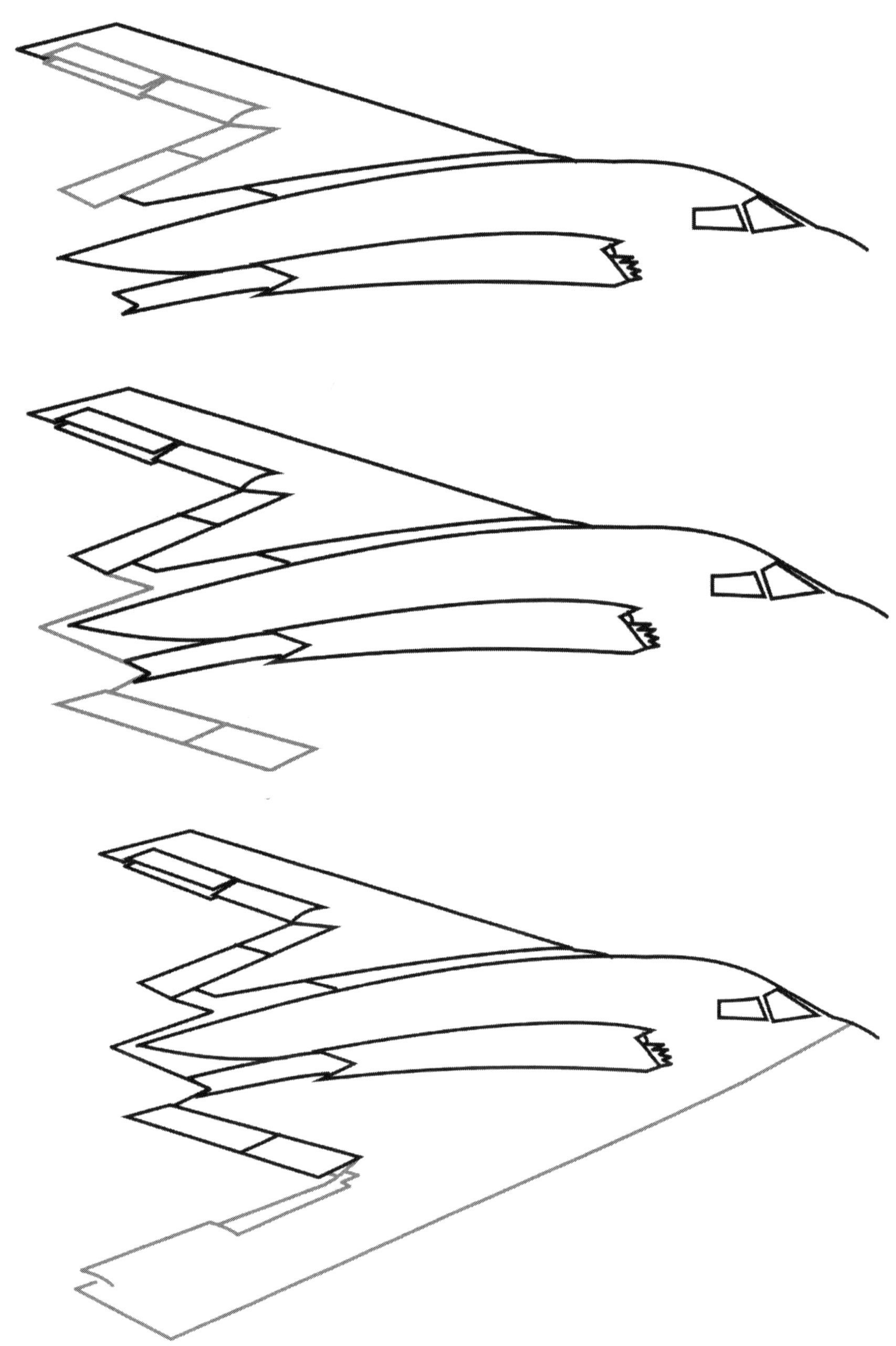

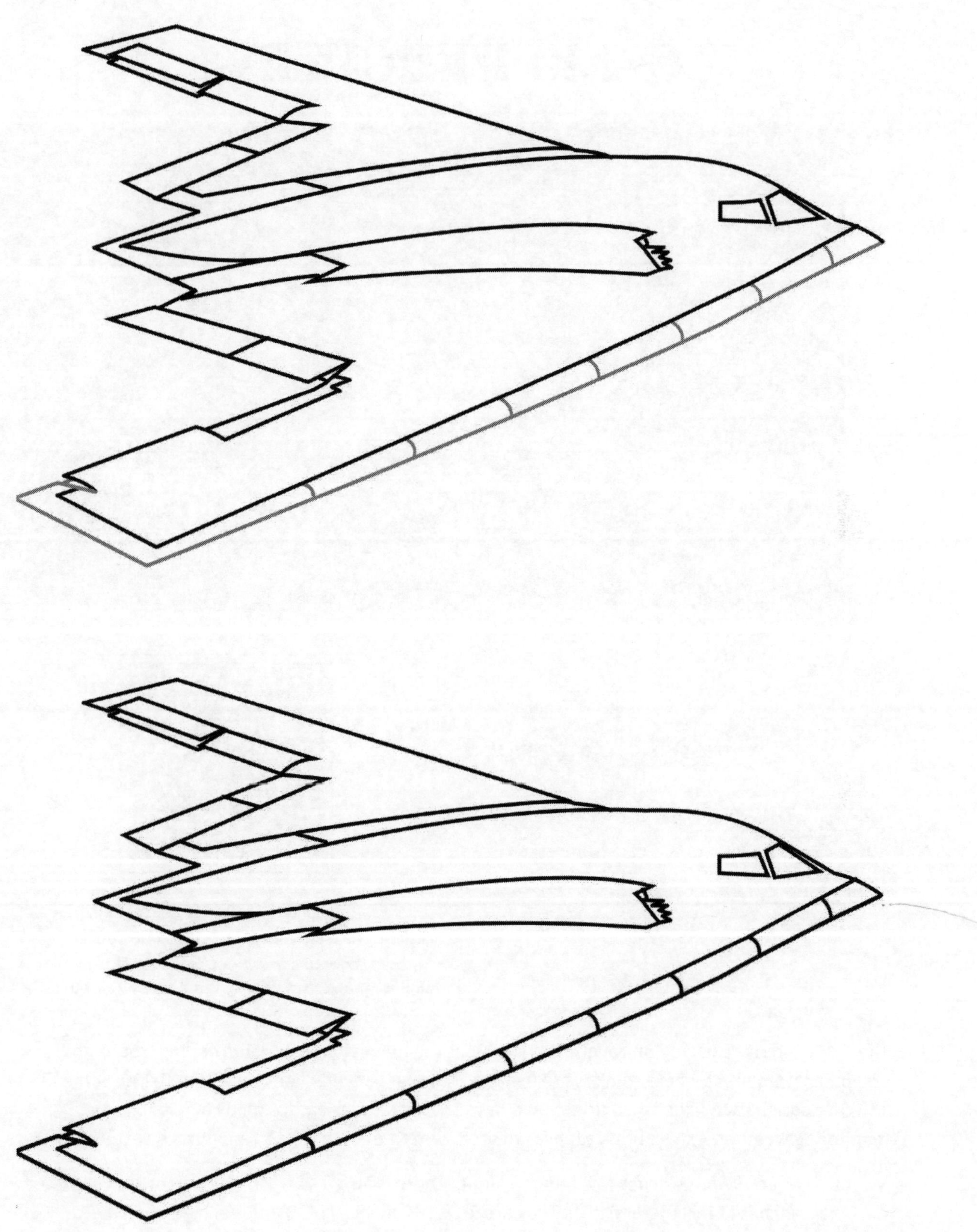

C-130 HERCULES

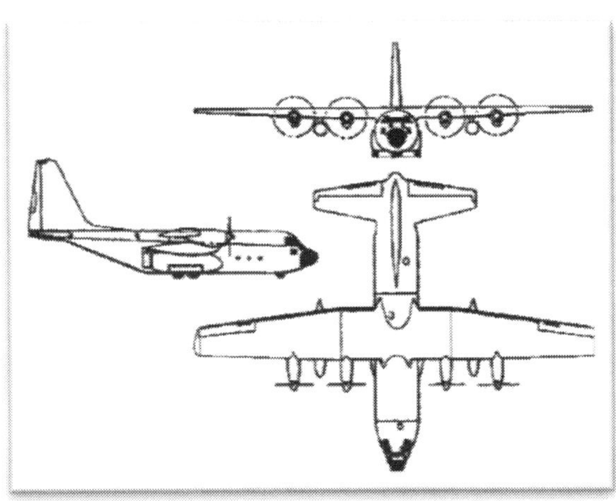

To see video of the C-130 in action,
click on the Quick Response (QR) code above or visit
https://www.dvidshub.net/video/297412/warex-global-medic-2013-misc-c-130-footage#.VcYSl_lViko

The C-130 aircraft can land on rough airstrips and is the main aircraft for airdropping troops and equipment into areas where soldiers are fighting. There are several versions of the C-130. Some C-130s are designed to fight forest fires. Some have special equipment for medical missions, or monitoring weather. Others bring supplies to areas where there has been a natural disaster.

Most C-130s are 97 ft., 9 inches (29.3 meters) long. There is also a "stretch" version of the C-130 that is 112 ft. 9 inches (34.69 meters) long. They are 38 ft., 10 inches (11. 9 meters) high and have a wingspan of 132 ft., 7 inches (39.7 meters). The fastest model of the C-130 can fly about 417 mph (Mach 0.59) at 22,000 ft. (6,706 meters).

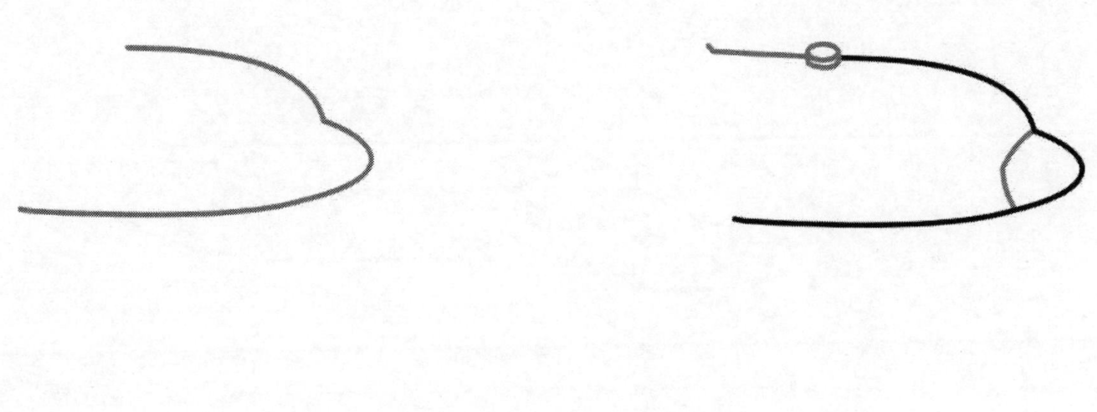

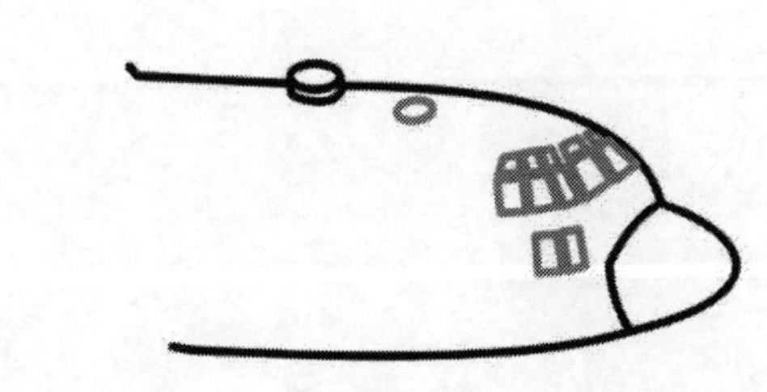

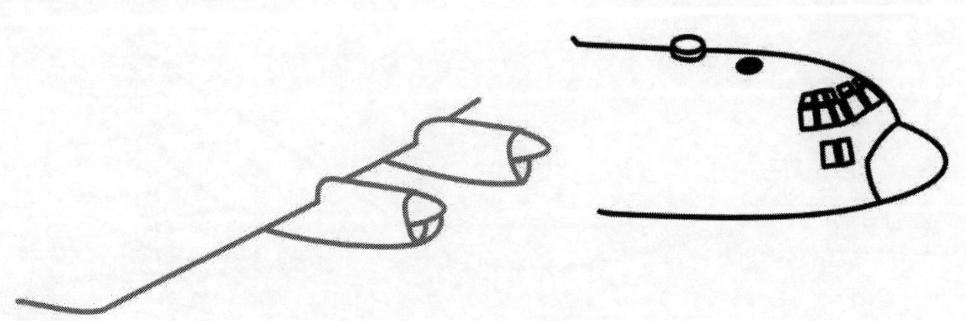

CH-47 CHINOOK

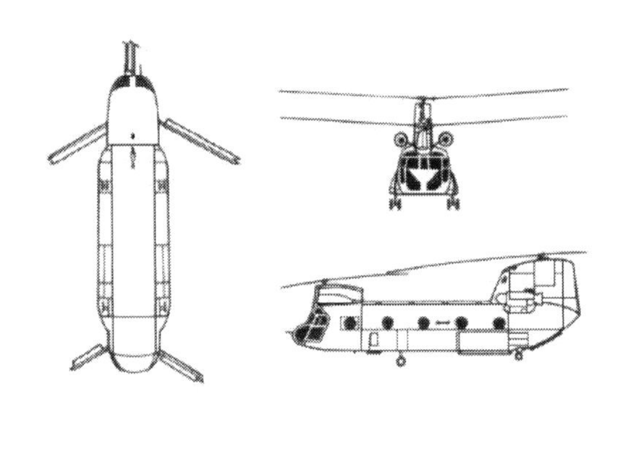

To see video of the CH-47 in action, click on the Quick Response (QR) code above or visit https://www.dvidshub.net/video/115468/ch-47-chinook-shots#.V0NygBU8KnN

The CH-47 is a heavy-lift helicopter whose primary job is to move troops and equipment to the battlefield. It can carry as many as 55 troops or 28,000 lbs. (12,700 kg) of cargo. The CH-47 also flies rescue and firefighting missions. The CH-47 has a crew of three (pilot, co-pilot and flight engineer) and a top speed of 196 mph (315 km/h). The body (fuselage) of the CH-47 is 52.0 ft. (15.9 m) long. The rotors extend past the body and counting the rotors, the CH-47 is 99.0 ft. (30.18 m) long. It's 18.92 ft. (5.77 m) high.

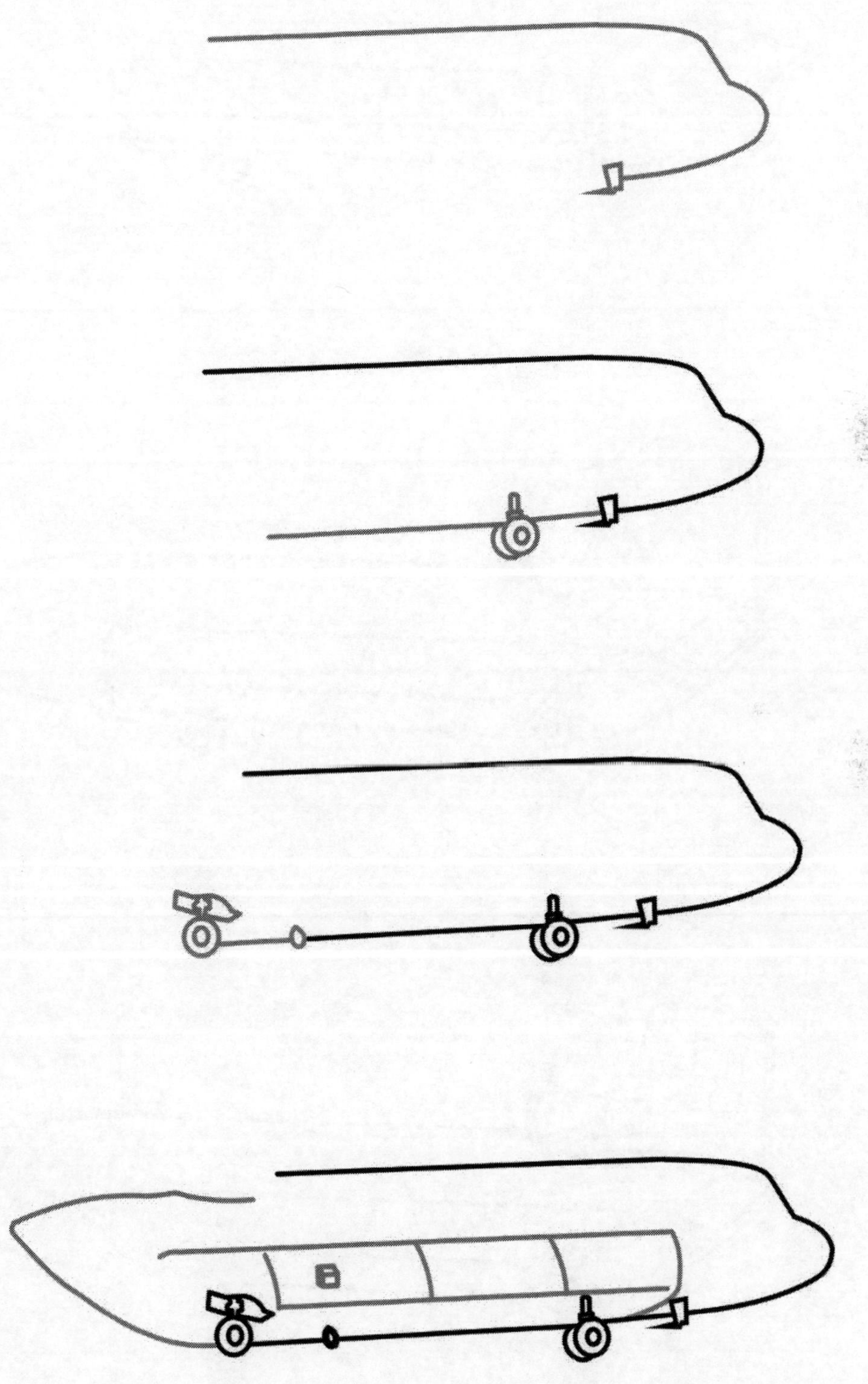

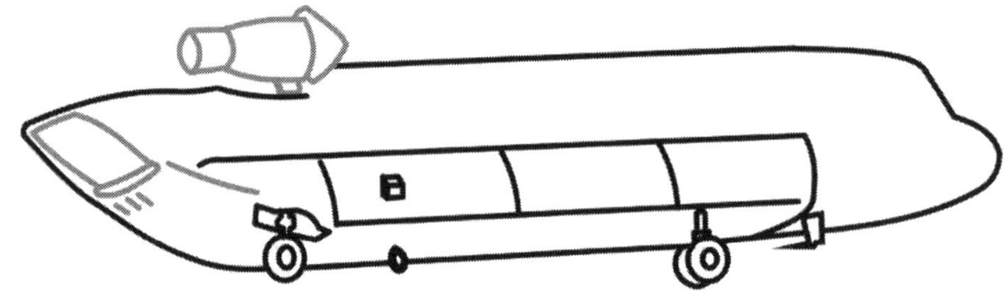

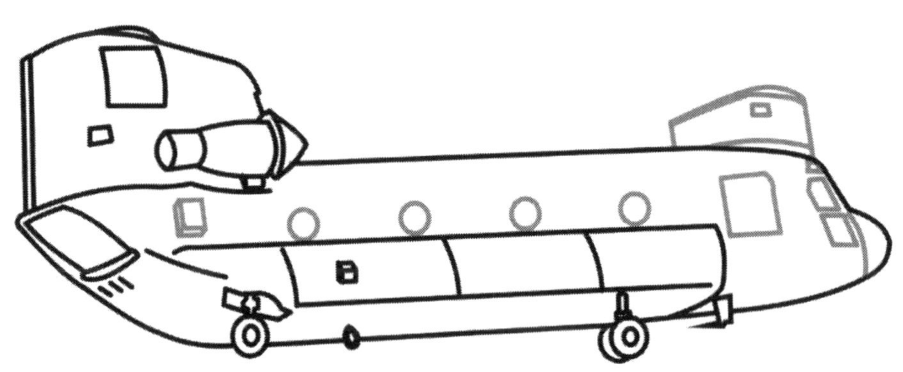

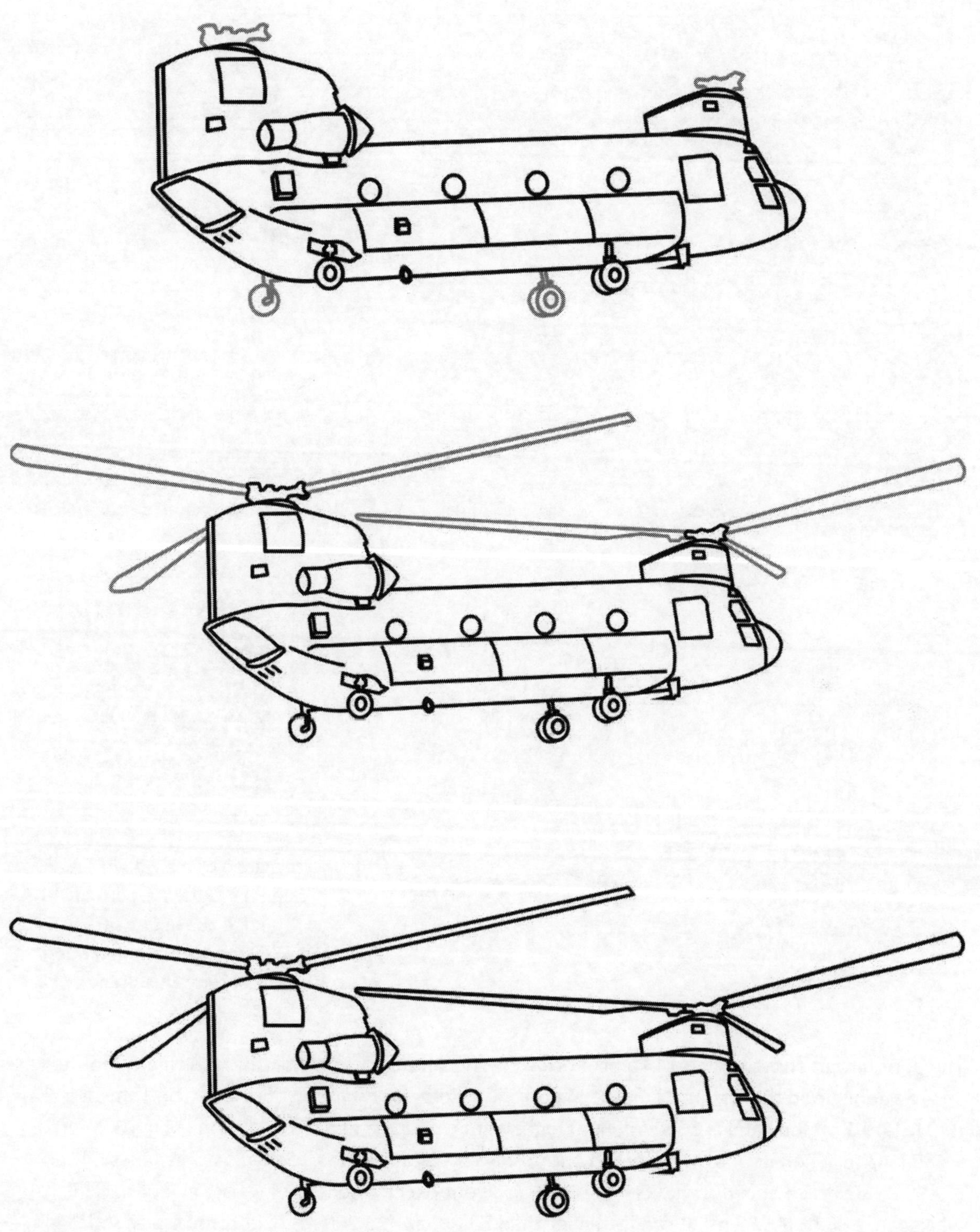

F-14 TOMCAT

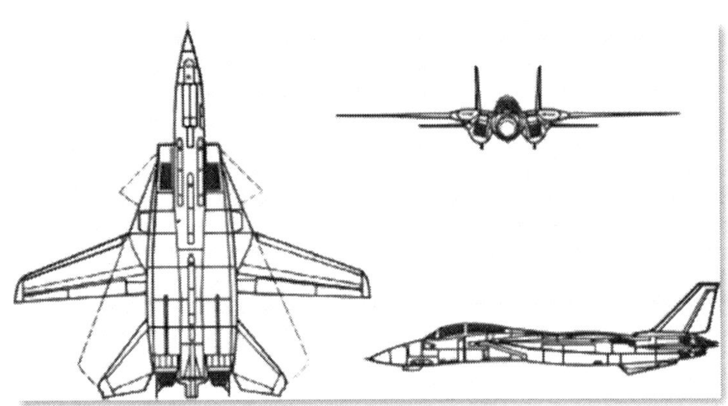

To see video of the F-14 in action, click on the Quick Response (QR) code above or visit https://www.dvidshub.net/video/10631/f-14-tomcats#.VcZnt_lViko

The photograph above is an F-14 Tomcat breaking the sound barrier. The blurry area around the F-14 is a vapor cloud that forms when the aircraft flies close to the speed of sound. The Tomcat is 62 ft. 9 in. (19.1 m) long and is 16 ft. (4.99 m) high. Its maximum speed is 1,544 mph (Mach 2.34 or 2,485 km/h). When its wings are spread out for low-speed flight, the Tomcat's wingspan is 64 ft. (19.55 m). For high-speed flight, its wings can be swept back. When its wings are swept back, its wingspan is 38 ft. (11.58 m). It can fly higher than 50,000 ft. (15,200 m). The Tomcat was retired in September, 2006. The Tomcat was replaced by the F-18 Super Hornet.

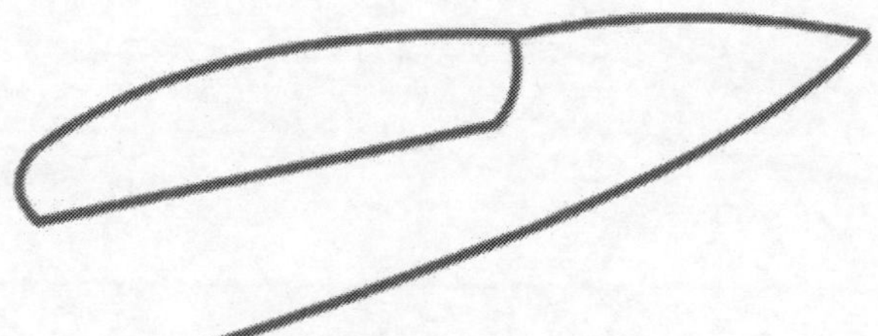

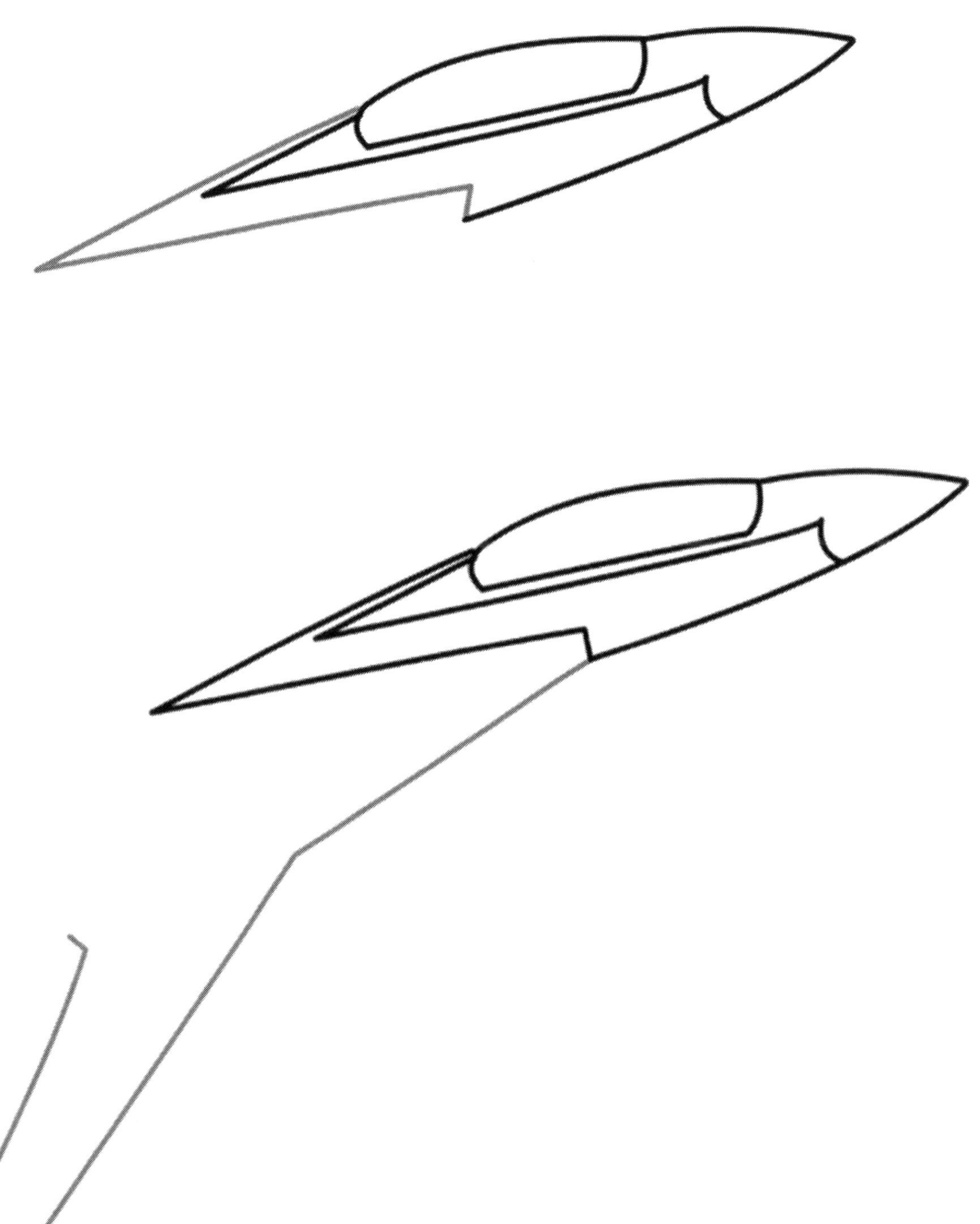

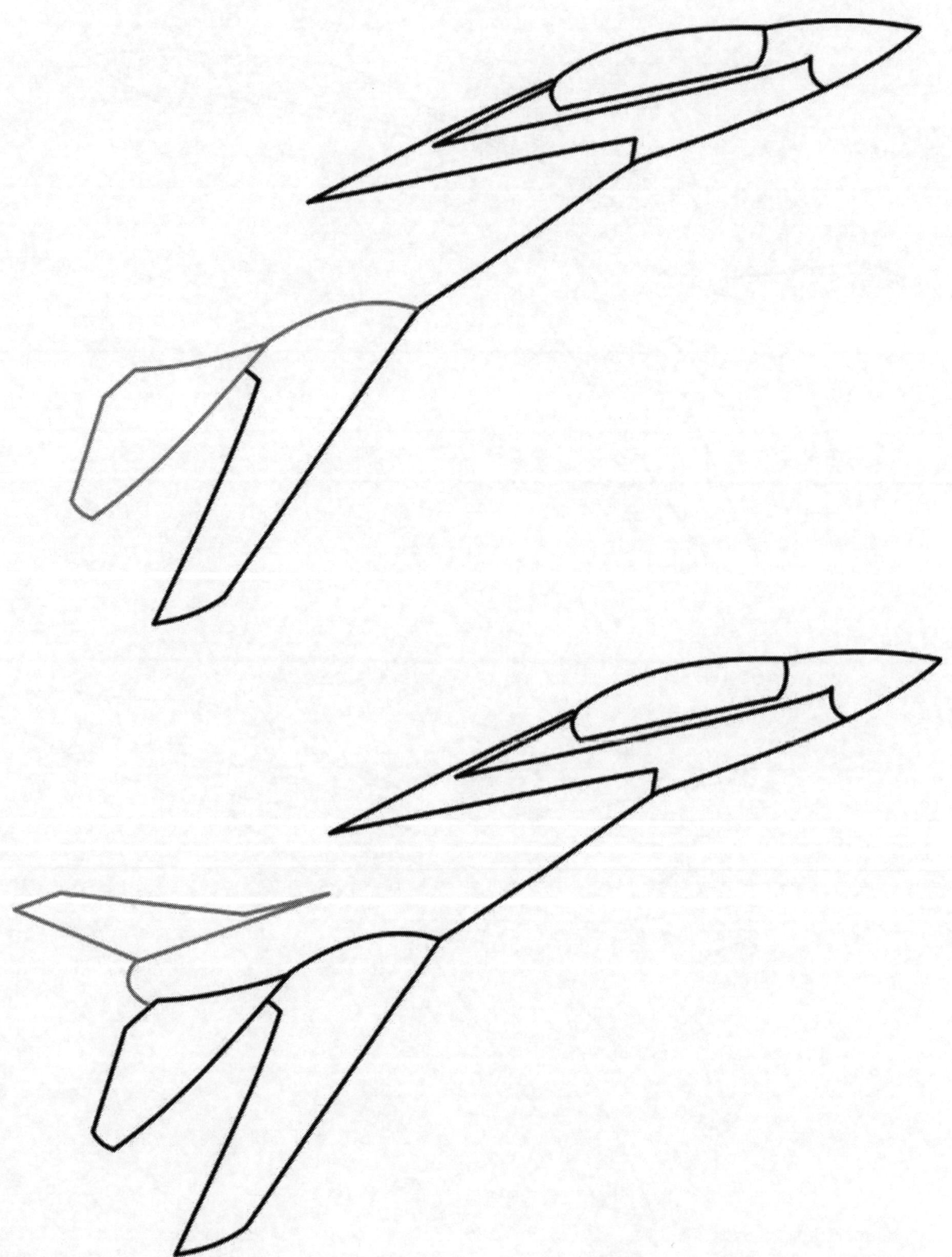

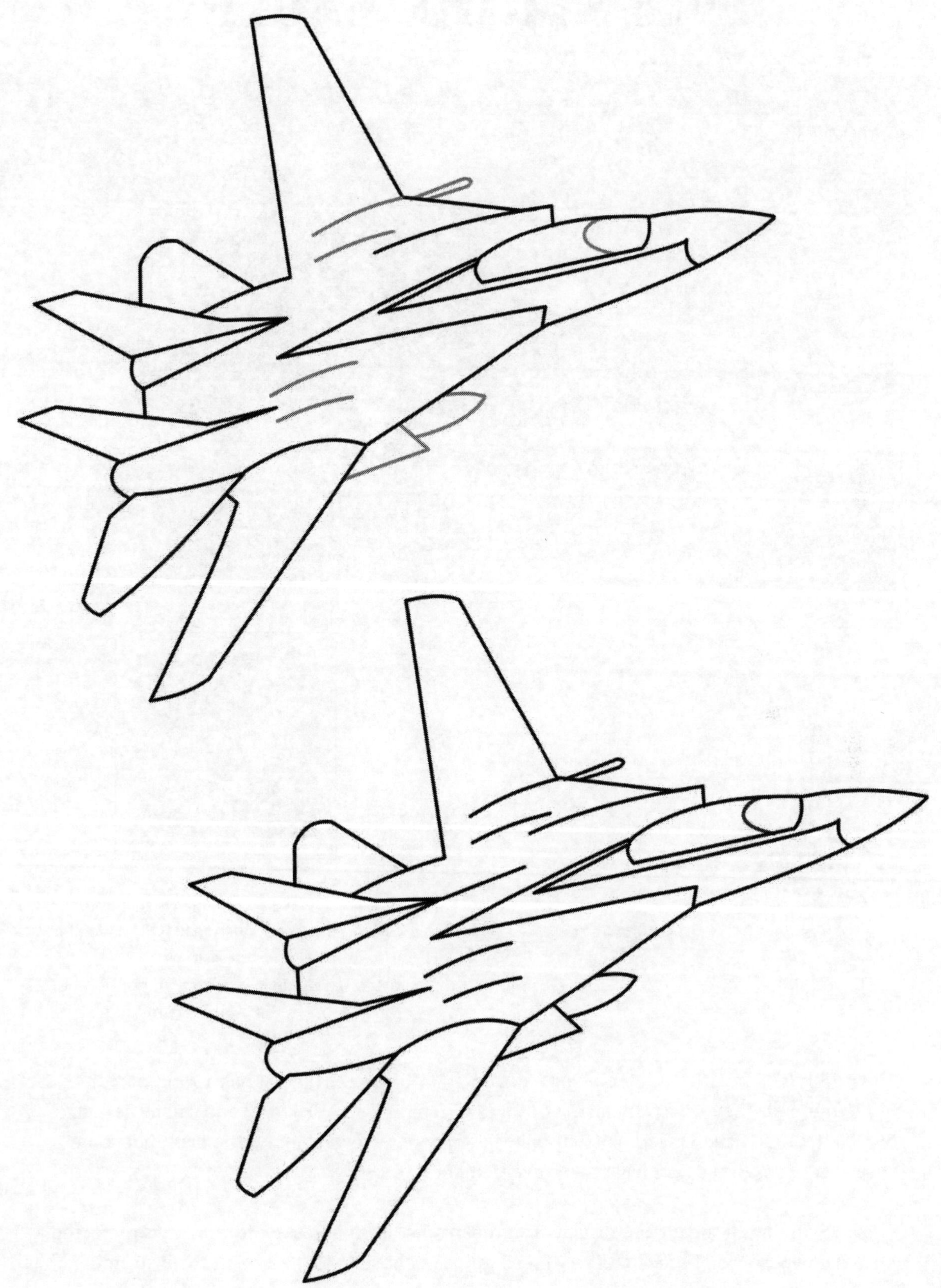

F-15 STRIKE EAGLE

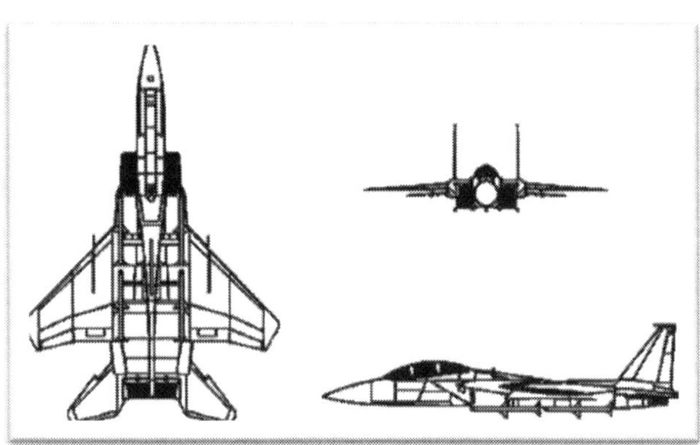

To see video of the F-15 in action,
click on the Quick Response (QR) code above
or visit
https://www.dvidshub.net/video/286960/f-15#.VcehfPlViko

The F-15 is 63.8 ft. (19.44 meters) long and 18.5 ft. (5.6 meters) high. It has a wingspan of 42.8 ft. (13 meters). The F-15 is very fast. It can fly 1,875 mph (3017.52 km/h) and can fly as high as 65,000 ft. (19,812 meters). The F-15 usually has only one crew member, the pilot, but some special versions of the F-15 have two crew members.

The F-15 also has a "heads-up" display. This means that all important information is projected onto the windshield of the aircraft so the pilot doesn't have to look down at the instruments.

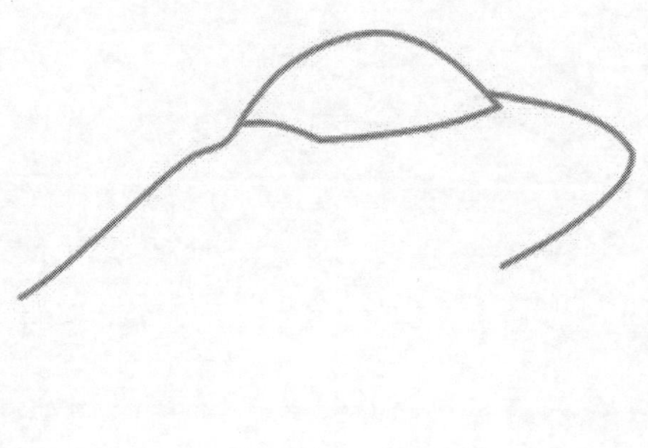

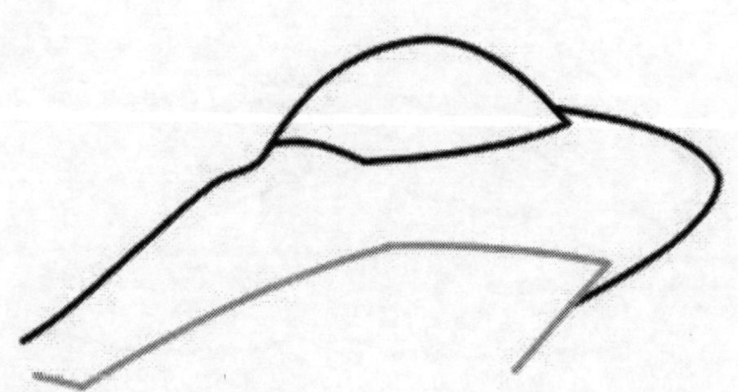

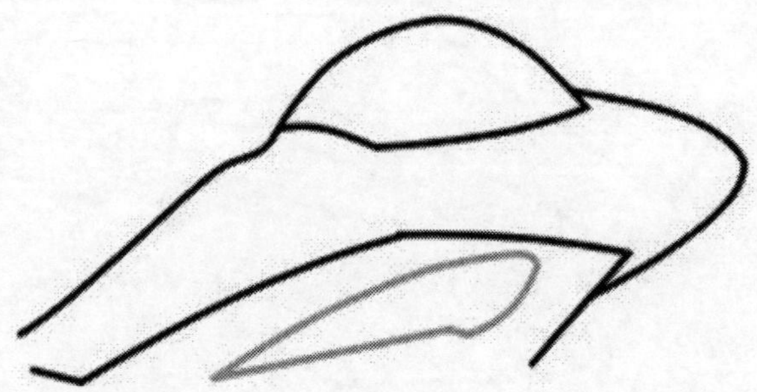

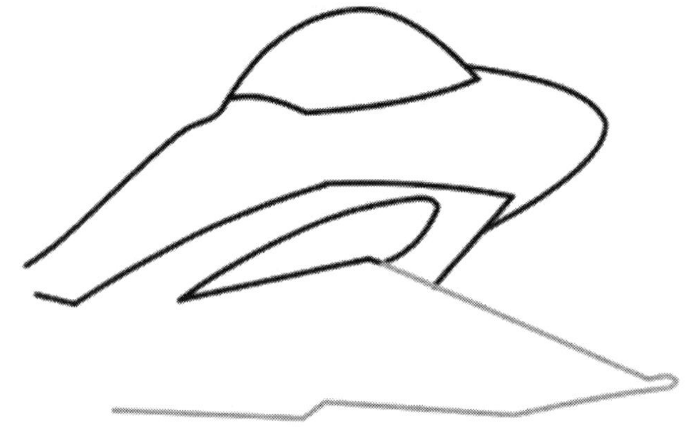

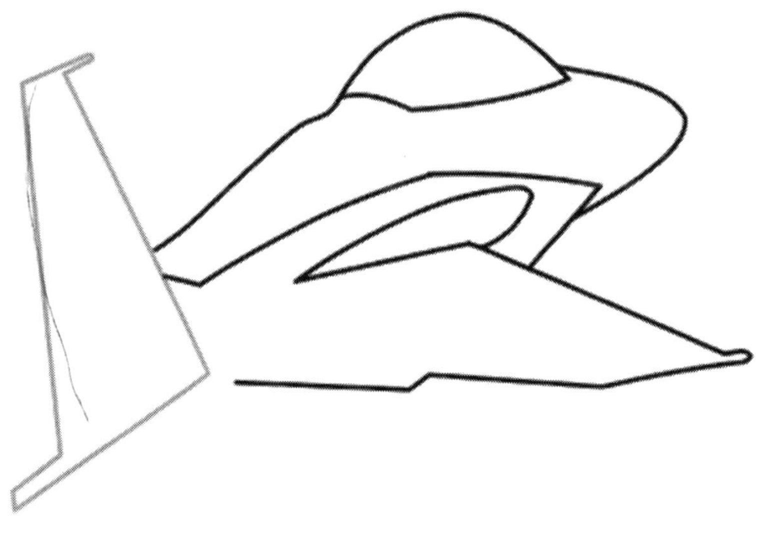

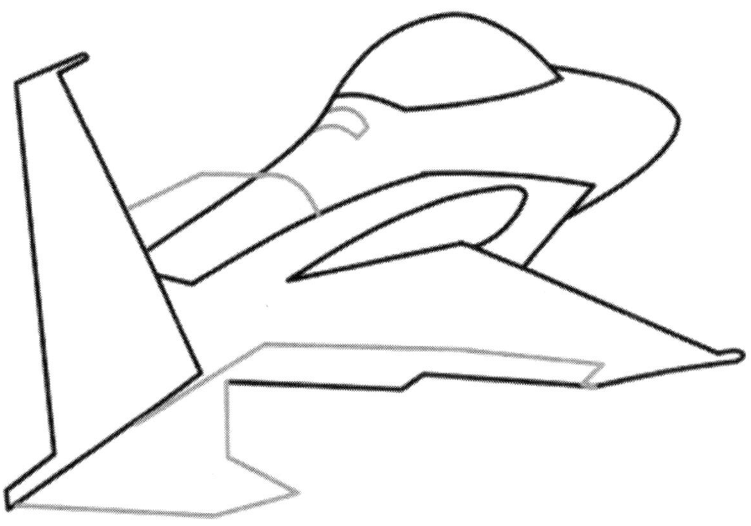

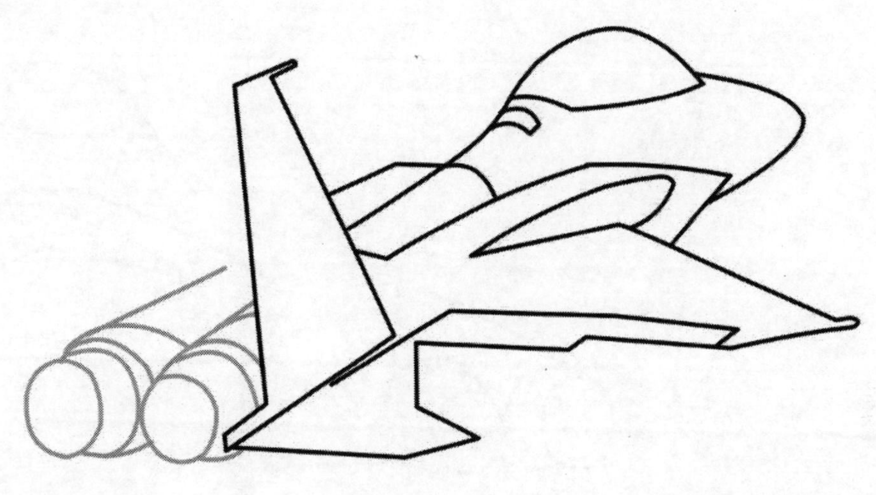

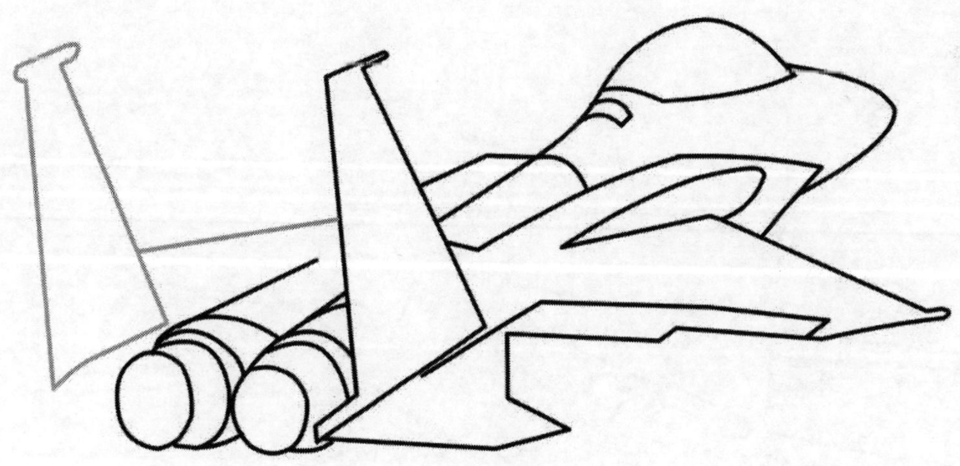

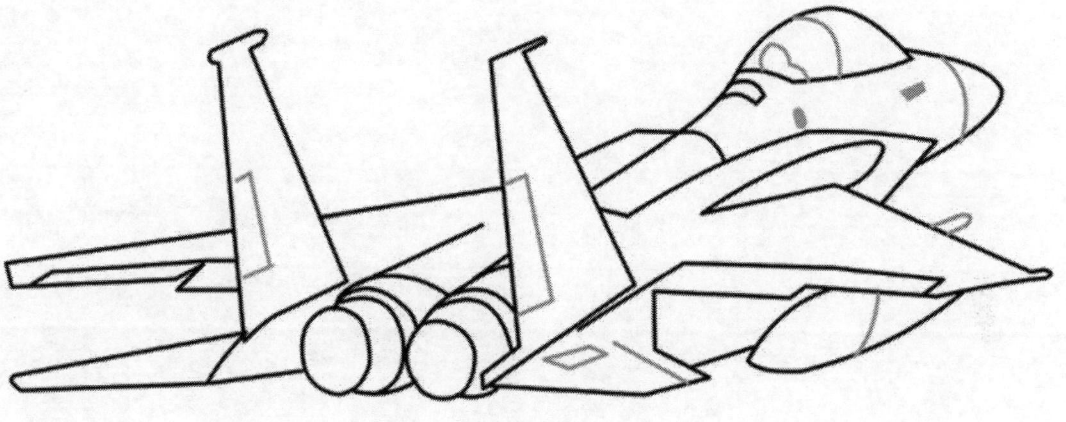

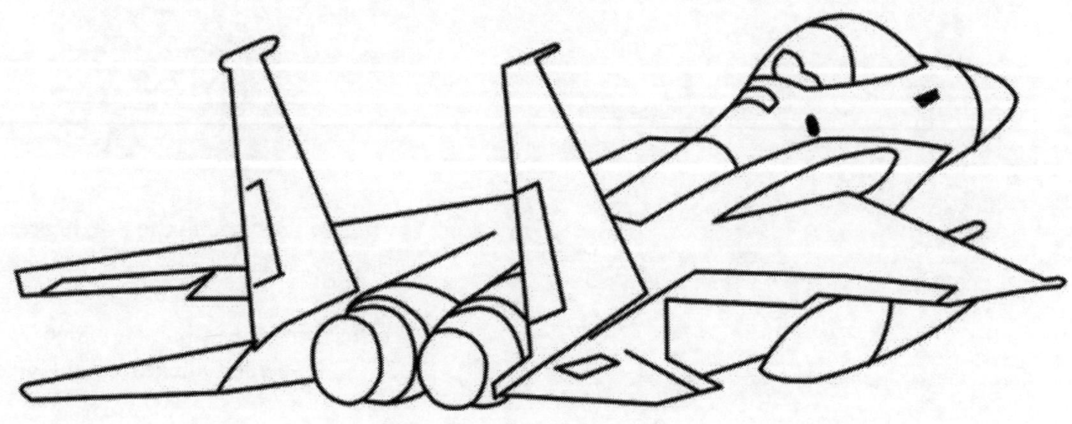

F-16 FIGHTING FALCON

To see video of the F-16 in action,
click on the Quick Response (QR) code above
or visit
https://www.dvidshub.net/video/254562/f-16-aerial-footage#.VcjQVPlViko

The F-16 is 49 ft. 5 in. (15.06 m) long and 16 ft. (4.88 m) high. Its wingspan is 32 ft. 8 in. (9.96 m). Its maximum speed is Mach 2 (1,320 mph, 2,120 km/h). The F-16 has a "bubble" canopy which makes it easier for the pilot to see in all directions. And the pilot's seat on reclines more than most other fighter jet seats to help the pilot stand high G-forces when the F-16 goes into a sharp turn. In September 2013, two US Air Force pilots controlled an unmanned F-16 from the ground and flew it over the Gulf of Mexico.

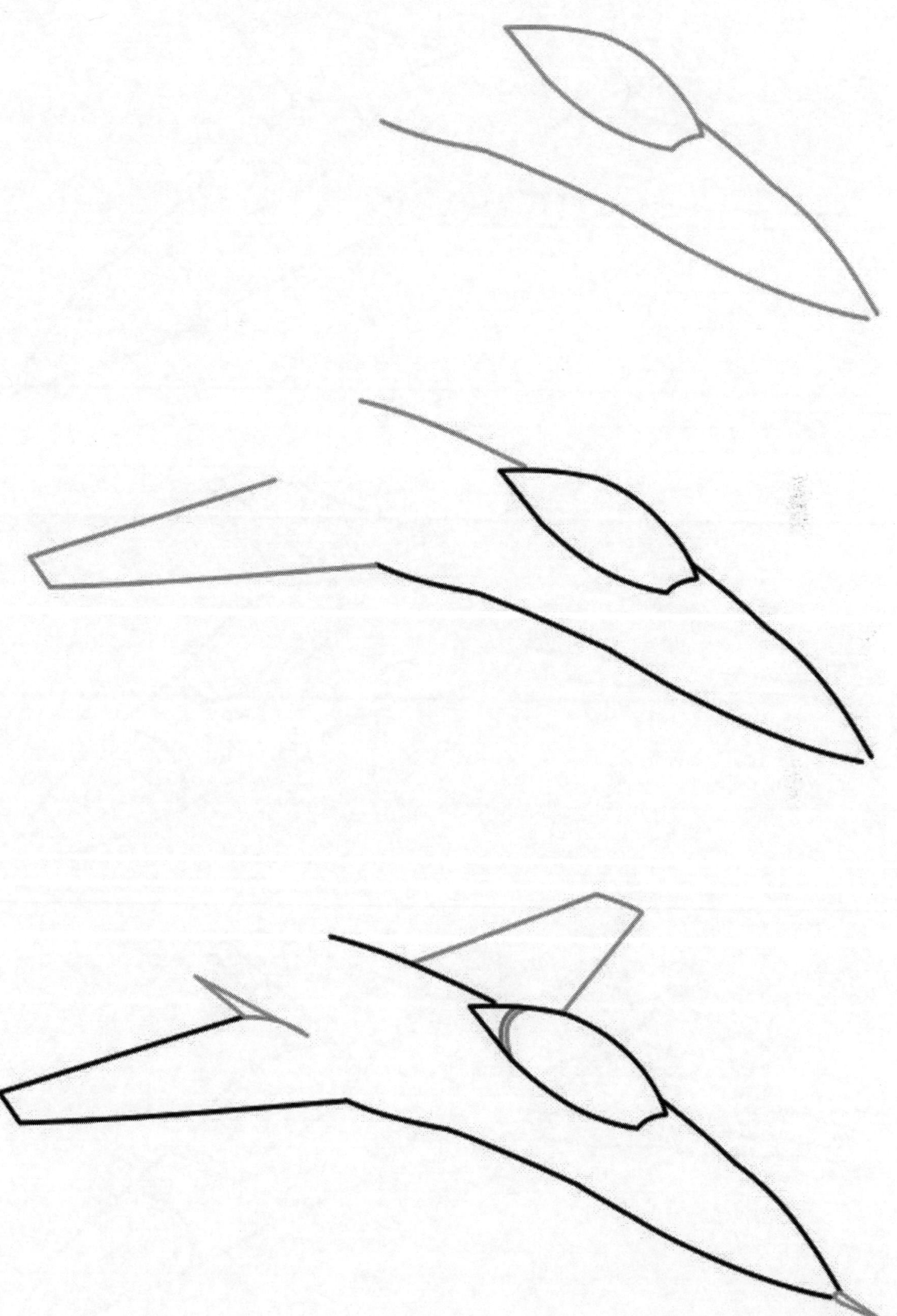

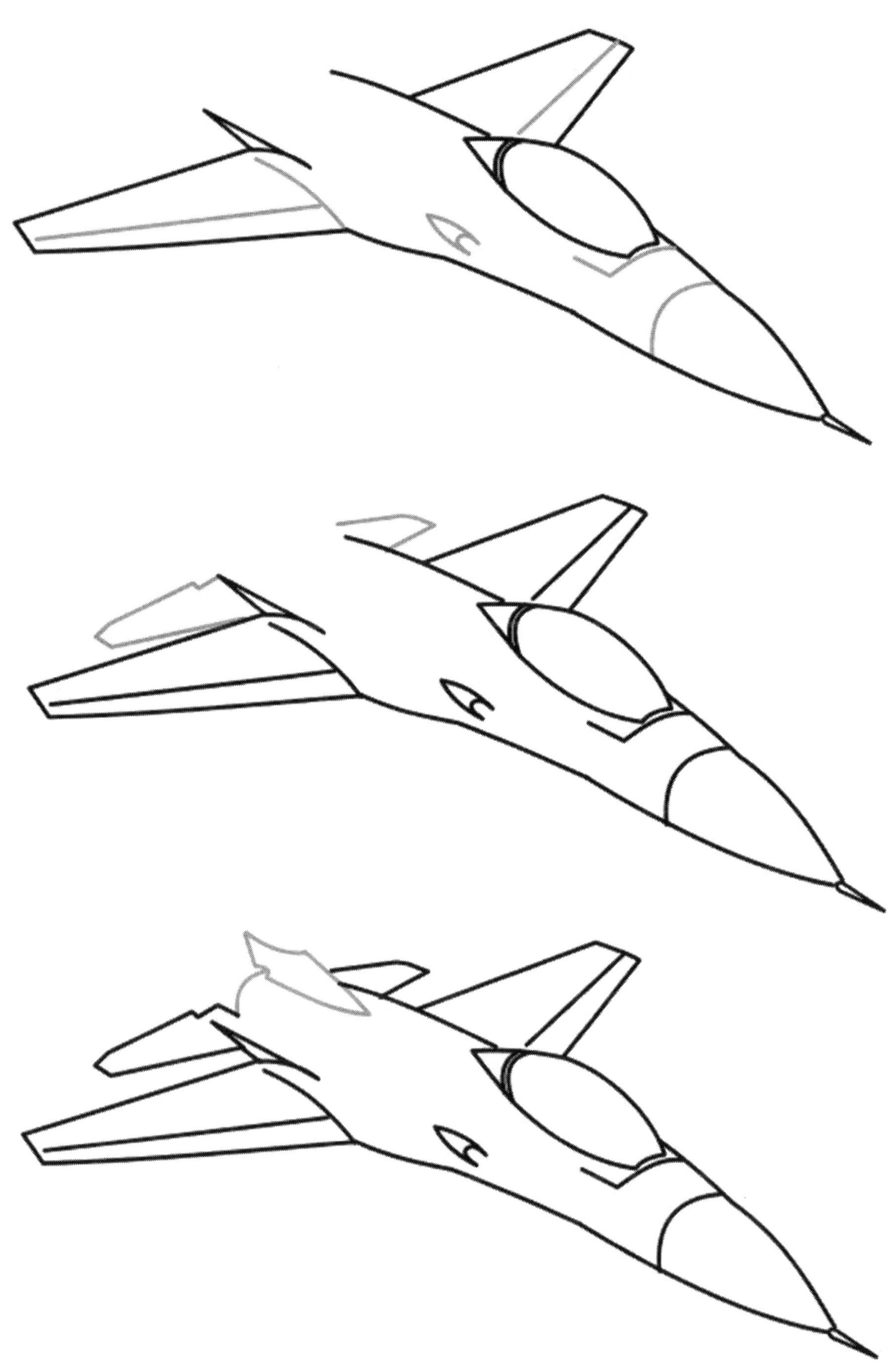

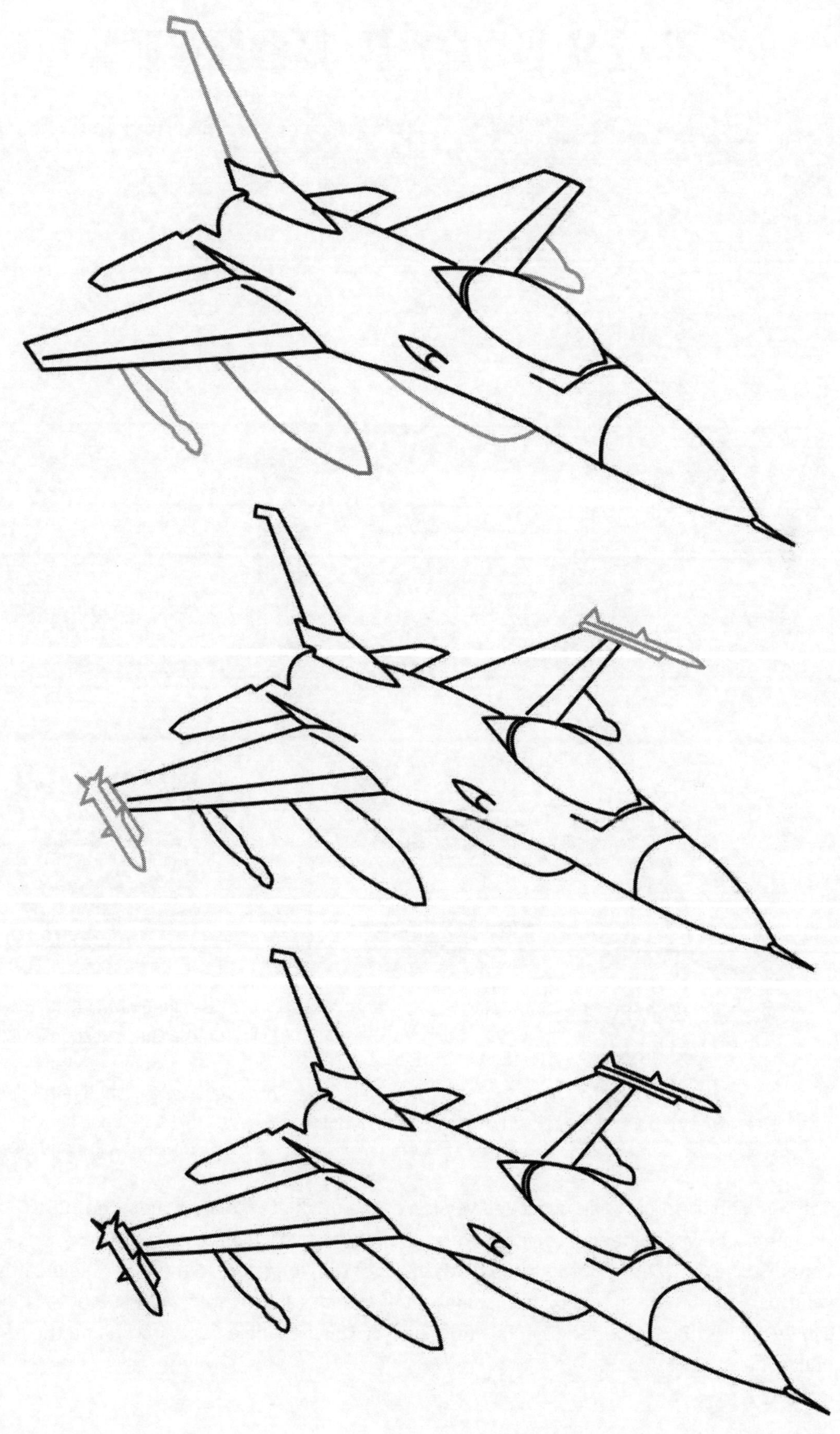

F-18 SUPER HORNET

To see video of the F-18 in action, click on the Quick Response (QR) code above or visit https://www.dvidshub.net/video/144148/f-18f-super-hornet-mission#.VczKe_lViko

The F-18 Super Hornet is an improved version of the original F/A-18 Hornet. The Super Hornet has newer flight electronics and displays for the pilot. It also has more advanced weapons systems. The F-18 Super Hornet is 60 ft, 1¼ in. (18.31 m) long and 16 ft. (4.88 m) high. It has a wingspan of 44 ft. 8½ in, (13.62 m). Its maximum speed is 1,190 mph (Mach 1.8 or 1,915 km/h). It can fly higher than 50,000 ft. (15,000+ m). The F/A-18E is a single-seat aircraft and the F/A-18F is built for a crew of two.

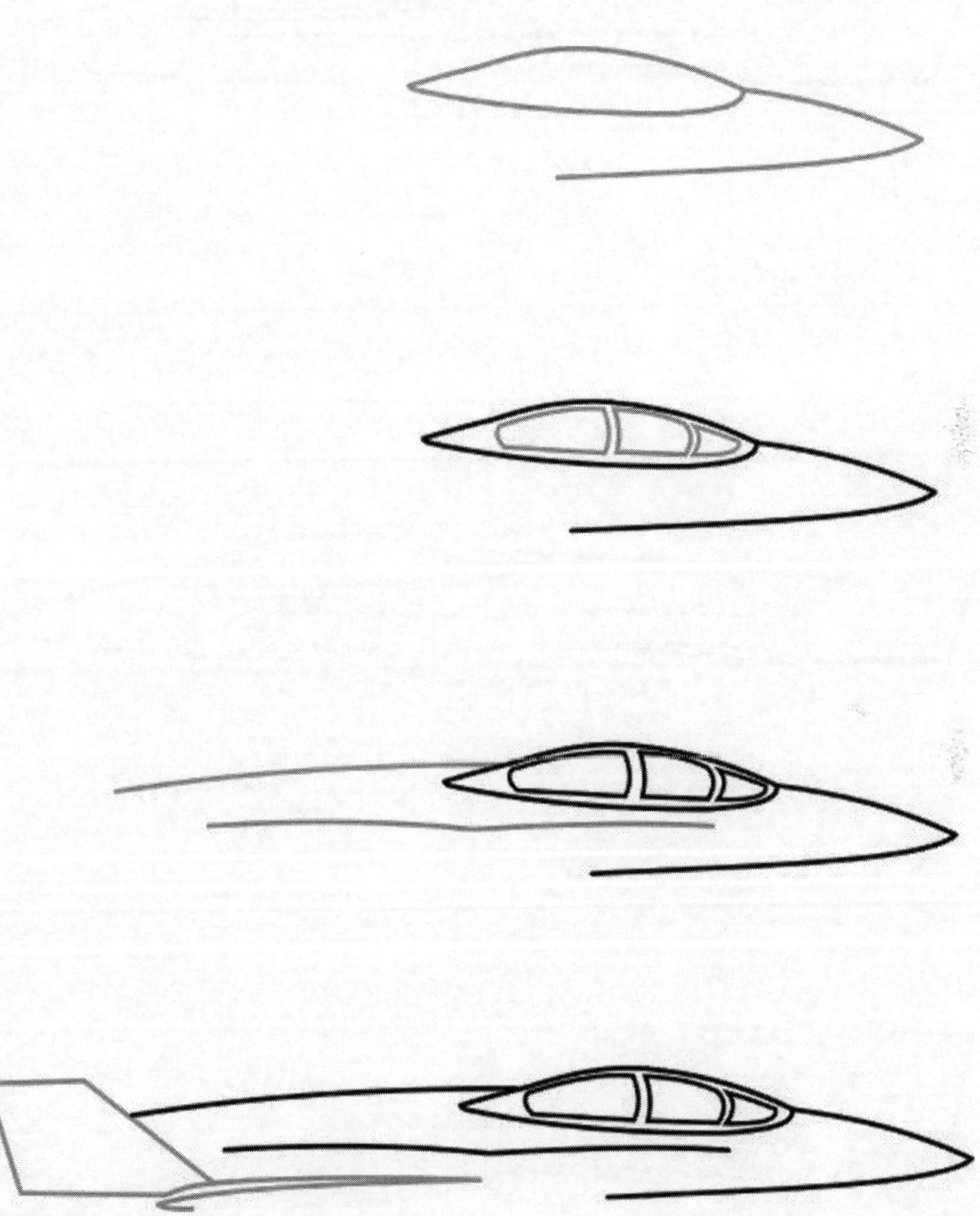

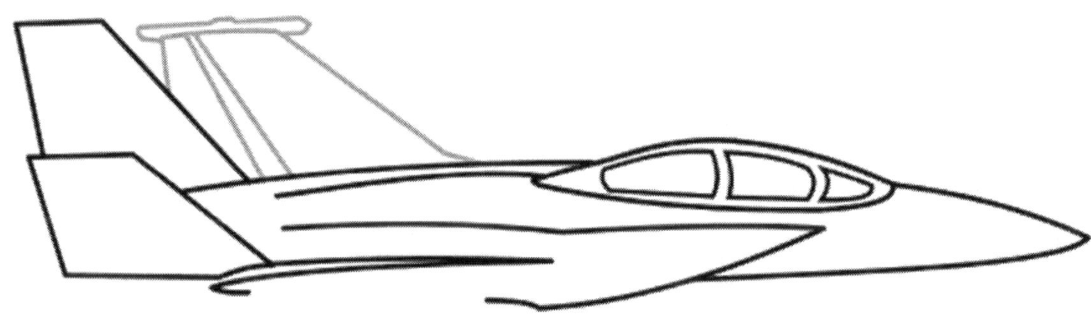

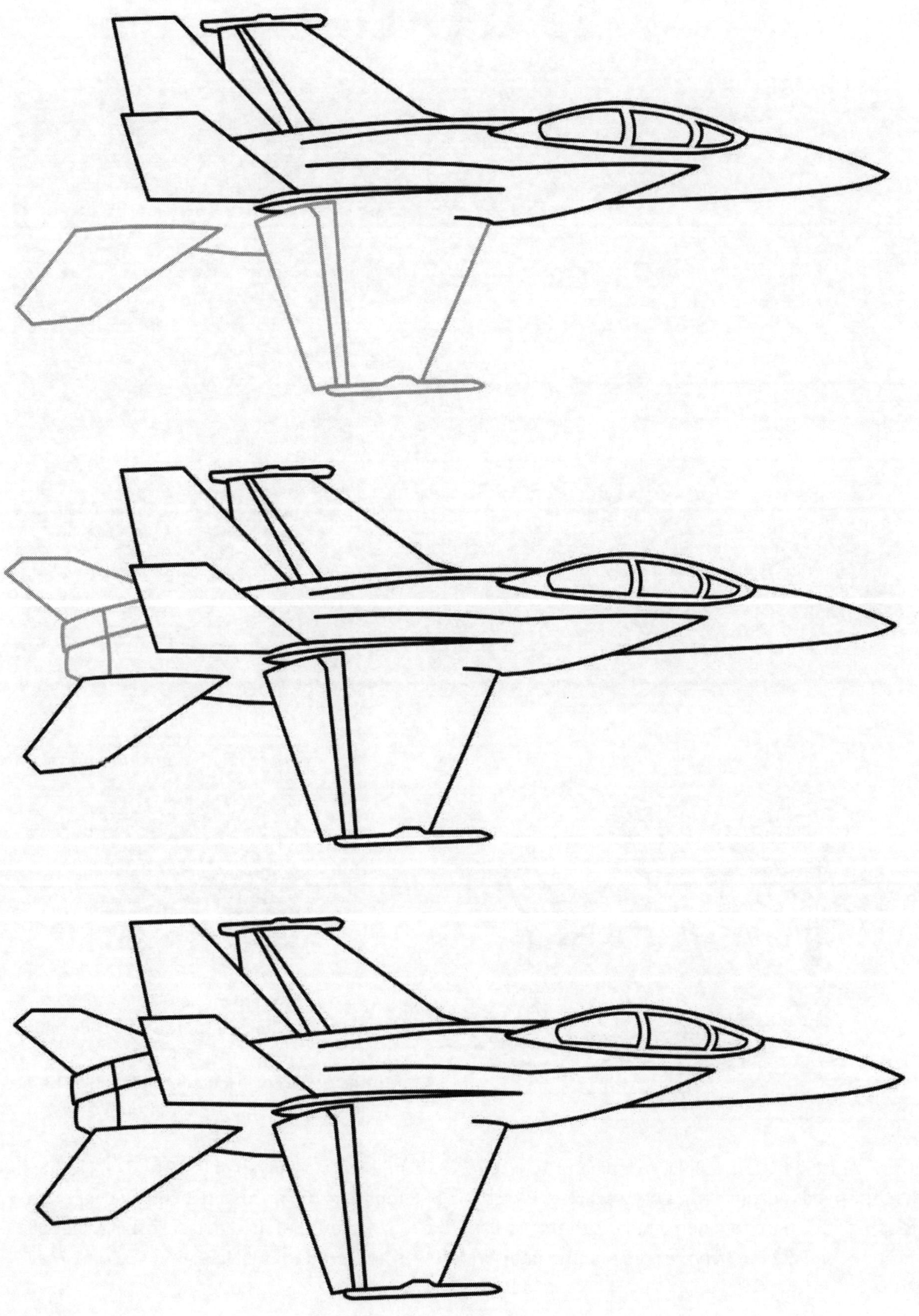

F-22 RAPTOR

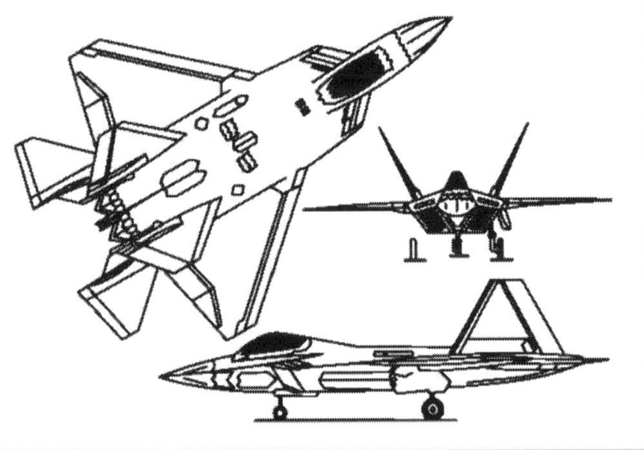

To see video of the F-22 in action,
click on the Quick Response (QR) code above
or visit
https://www.dvidshub.net/video/395413/air-force-tech-report-f-22-raptor#.VcjflvlViko

The F-22 is 62 ft. 1 in. (18.92 m) long and 16 ft. 8 in. (5.08 m) high. Its wingspan is 44 ft. 6 in. (13.56 m). Its top speed is estimated to be Mach 2.25 which is 1,500 mph (2,410 km/h) and it can fly over 65,000 feet high. It's hard for enemy radar systems to track the F-22 because of its radar-absorbing, metallic "skin." The F-22 has been retired and the final aircraft was delivered to the U. S. Air Force on 2 May 2012.

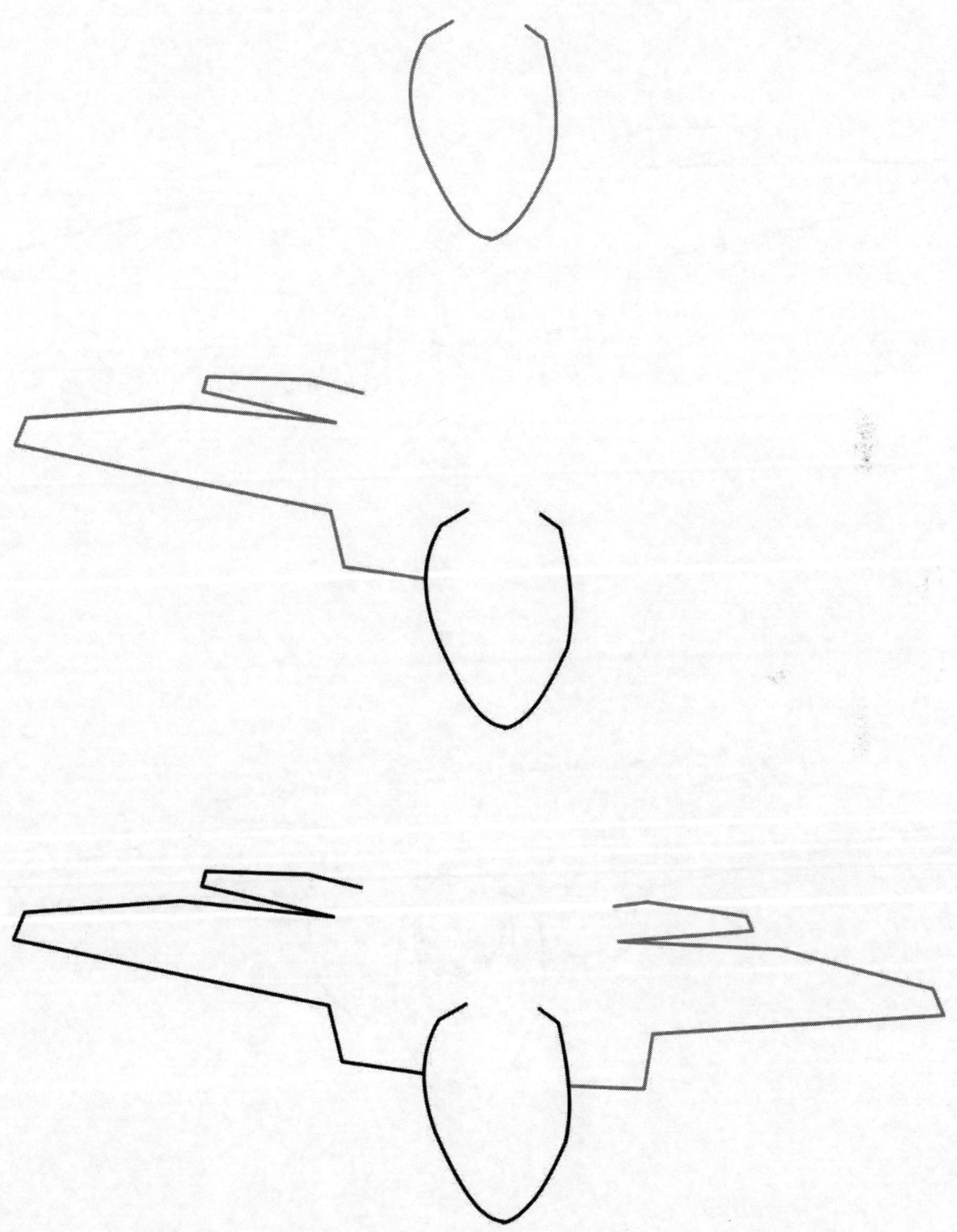

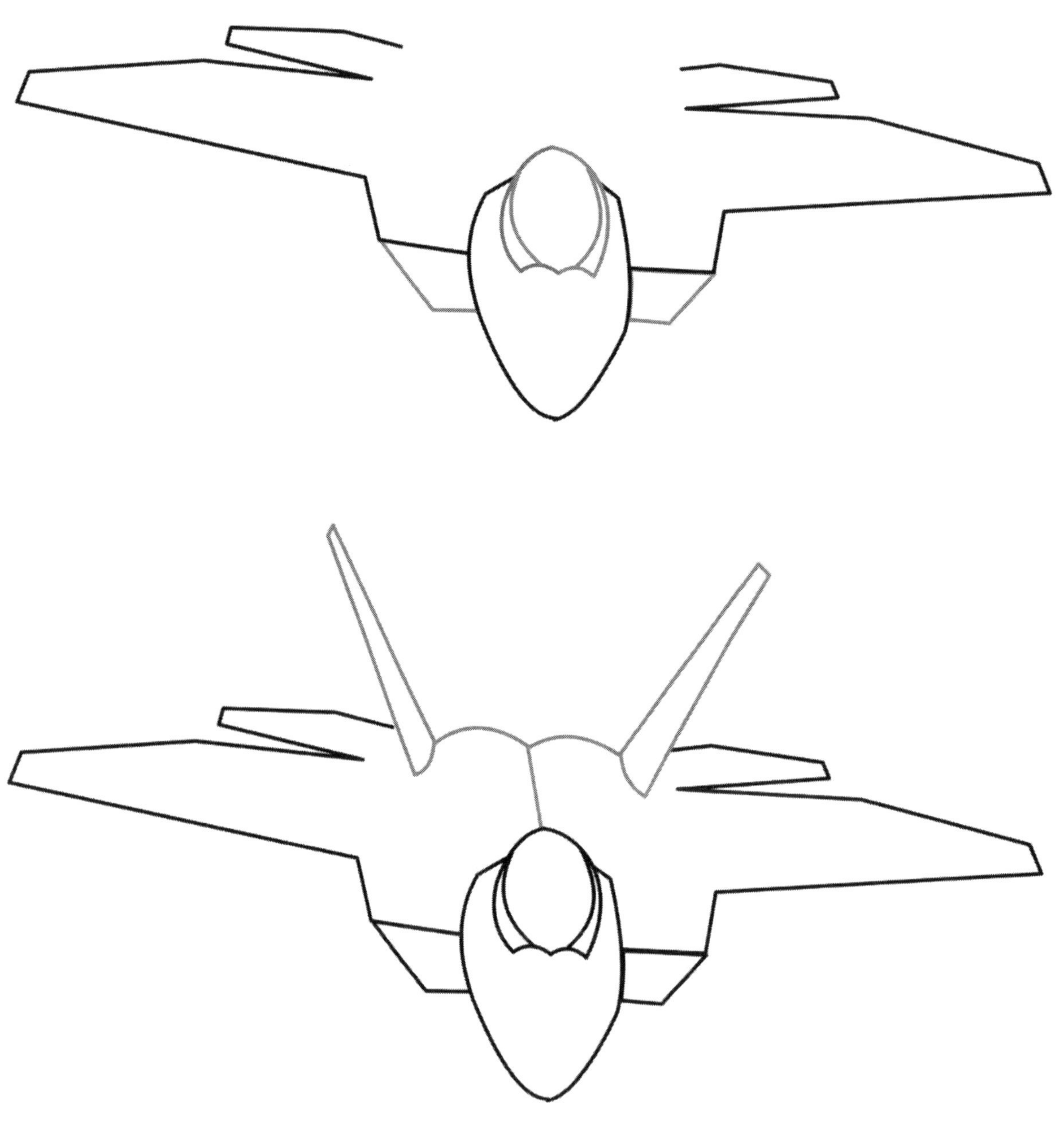

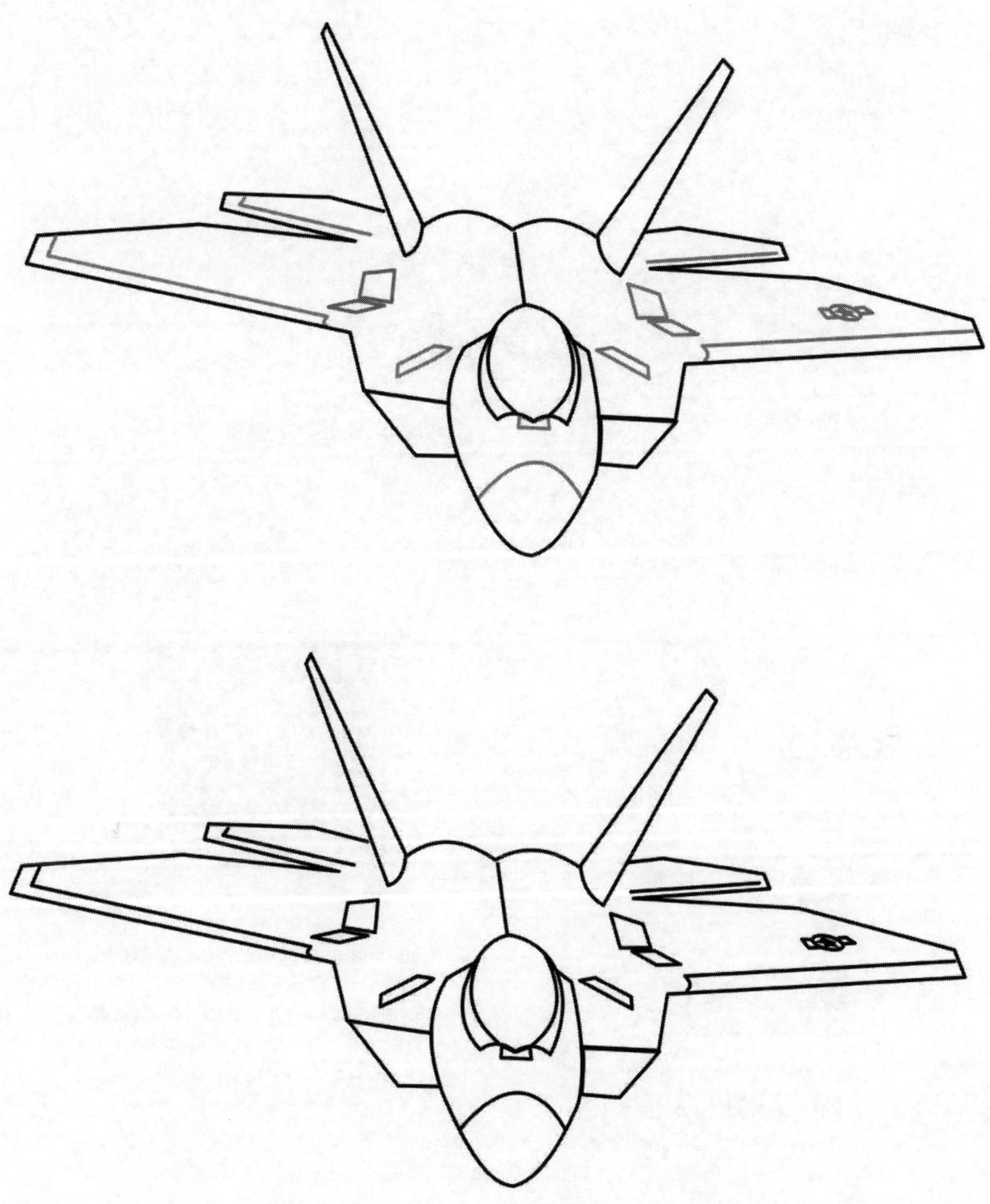

F-35 LIGHTNING II

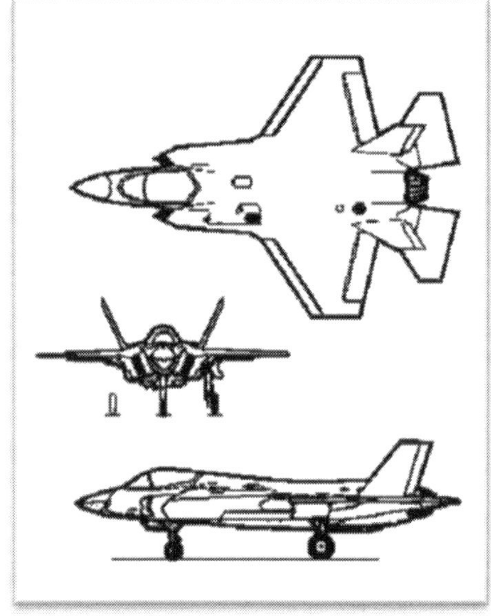

To see video of the F-35 in action,
Click on the Quick Response (QR) code
above or visit
https://www.dvidshub.net/video/41148
7/inaugural-f-35b-ski-jump-launch-
makes-history#.VcowpflViko

There are three models of the F-35:
The F-35A which takes off and lands on a runway like a typical jet fighter.
The F-35B which can take off vertically (straight up) or in a very short distance.
The F-35C which is designed to take off and land on aircraft carriers.

The F-35 is 50.5 ft. (15.67 m) long, 14.2 ft. (4.33 m) high and has a wingspan of 35 ft. (10.7 m). Its maximum speed is 1,200 mph (Mach 1.6 or 1,930 km/h) and it has a crew of one.

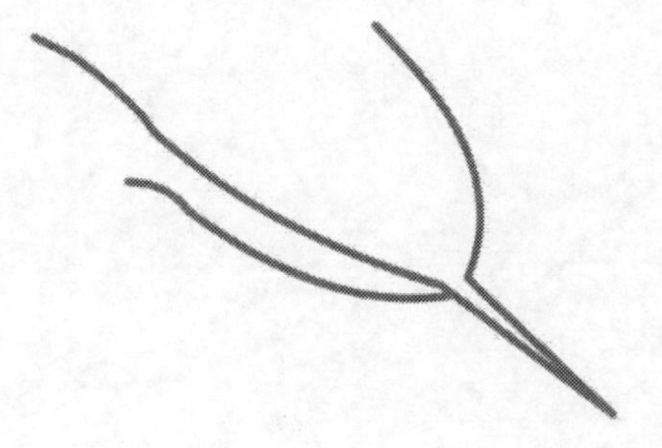

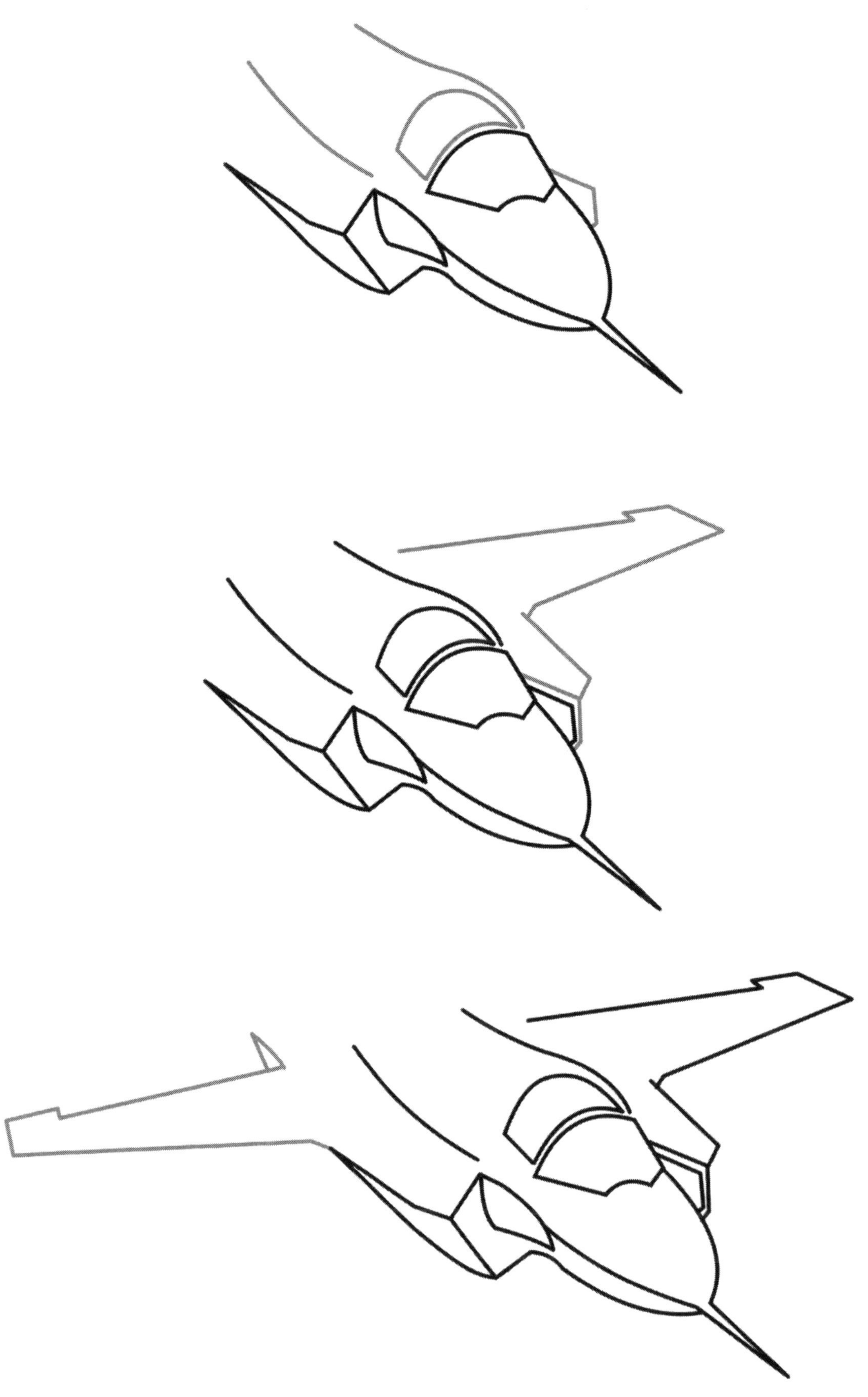

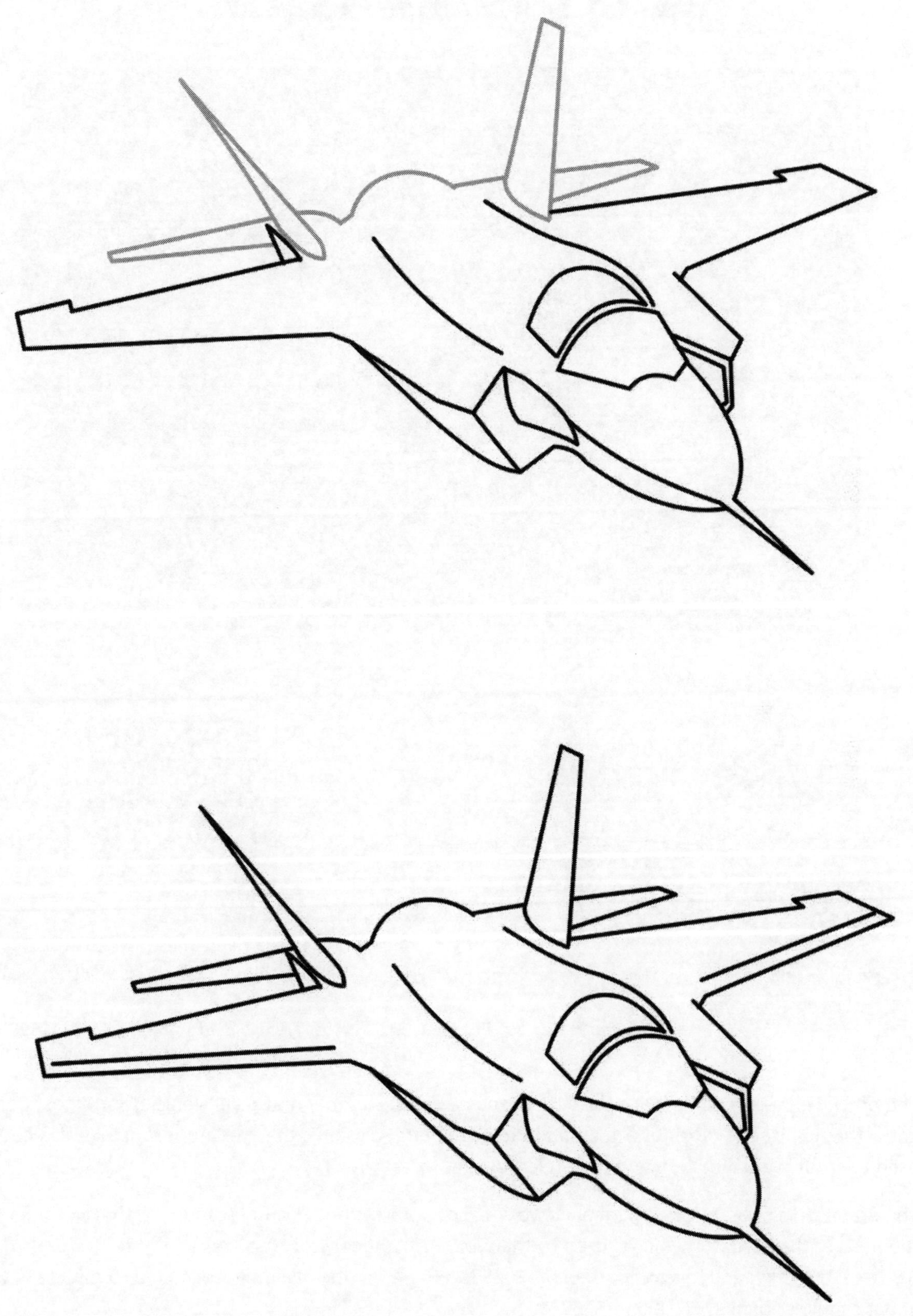

MQ-1 PREDATOR

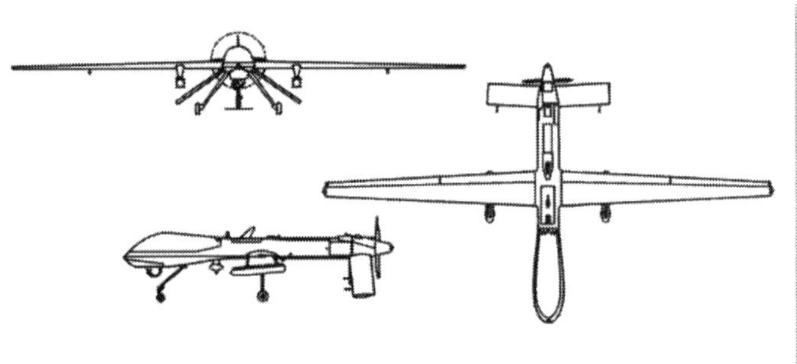

To see video of the MQ-1B in action,
Click on the Quick Response (QR) code above
or visit
https://www.dvidshub.net/video/418985/mq-1-predators-take-off-and-land#.Vcz8zPlViko

The official name for aircraft like the MQ-1 Predator is an, "unmanned aerial vehicle," but most people know them better as, "drones." In addition to its military missions, the Predator drone has also been used to study wind direction and other elements of forest fires.

The Predator is operated by a pilot and two sensor operators at a ground station. There is a camera in the nose of the Predator which is used by the pilot for flight control. The Predator is 27 ft. (8.22 m) long, 6.9 ft. (2.1 m) high and has a wingspan of 55.25 ft. (16.84 m). Its maximum speed is 135 mph (217 km/h) and it can fly as high as 25,000 ft. (7,620 m).

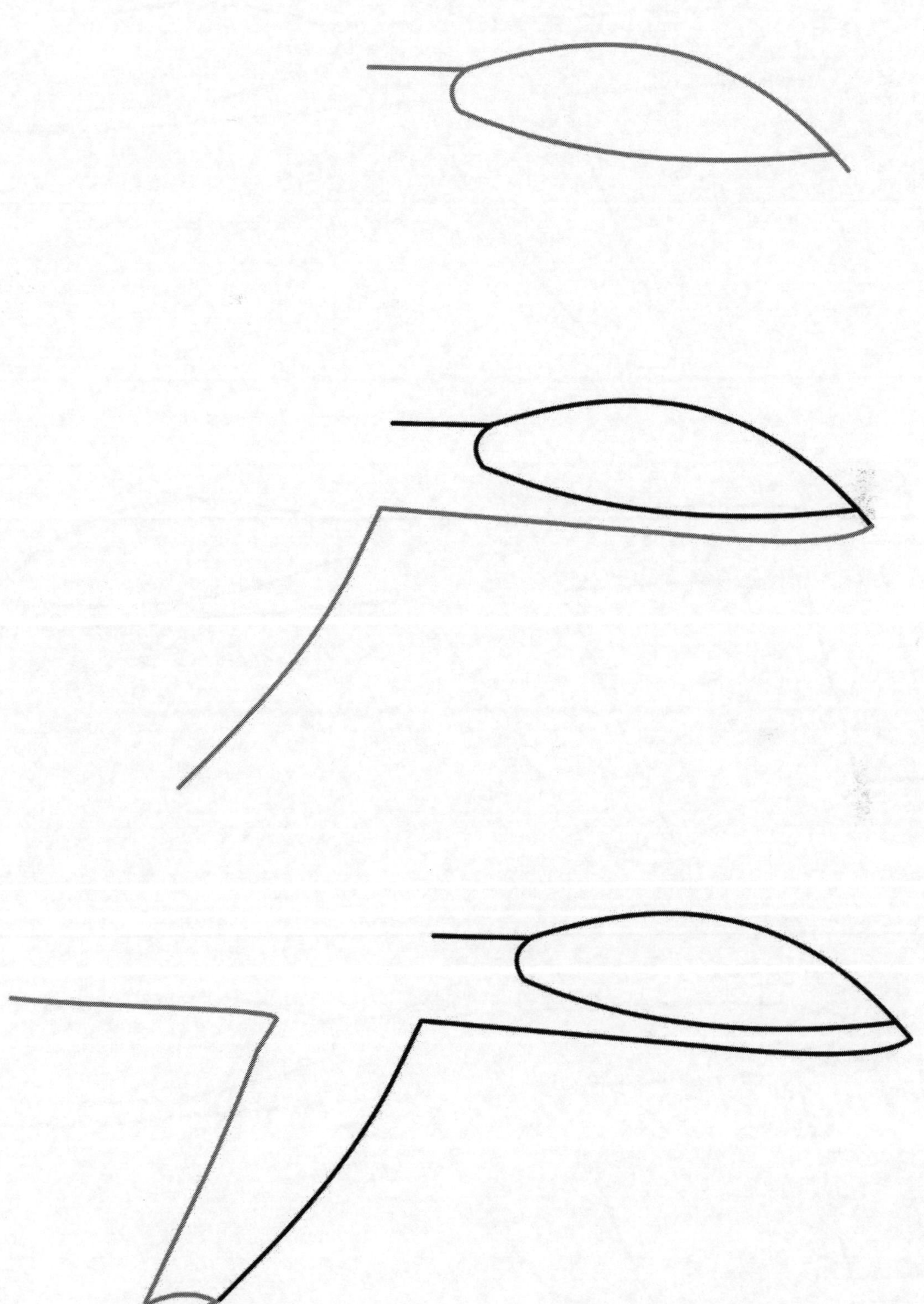

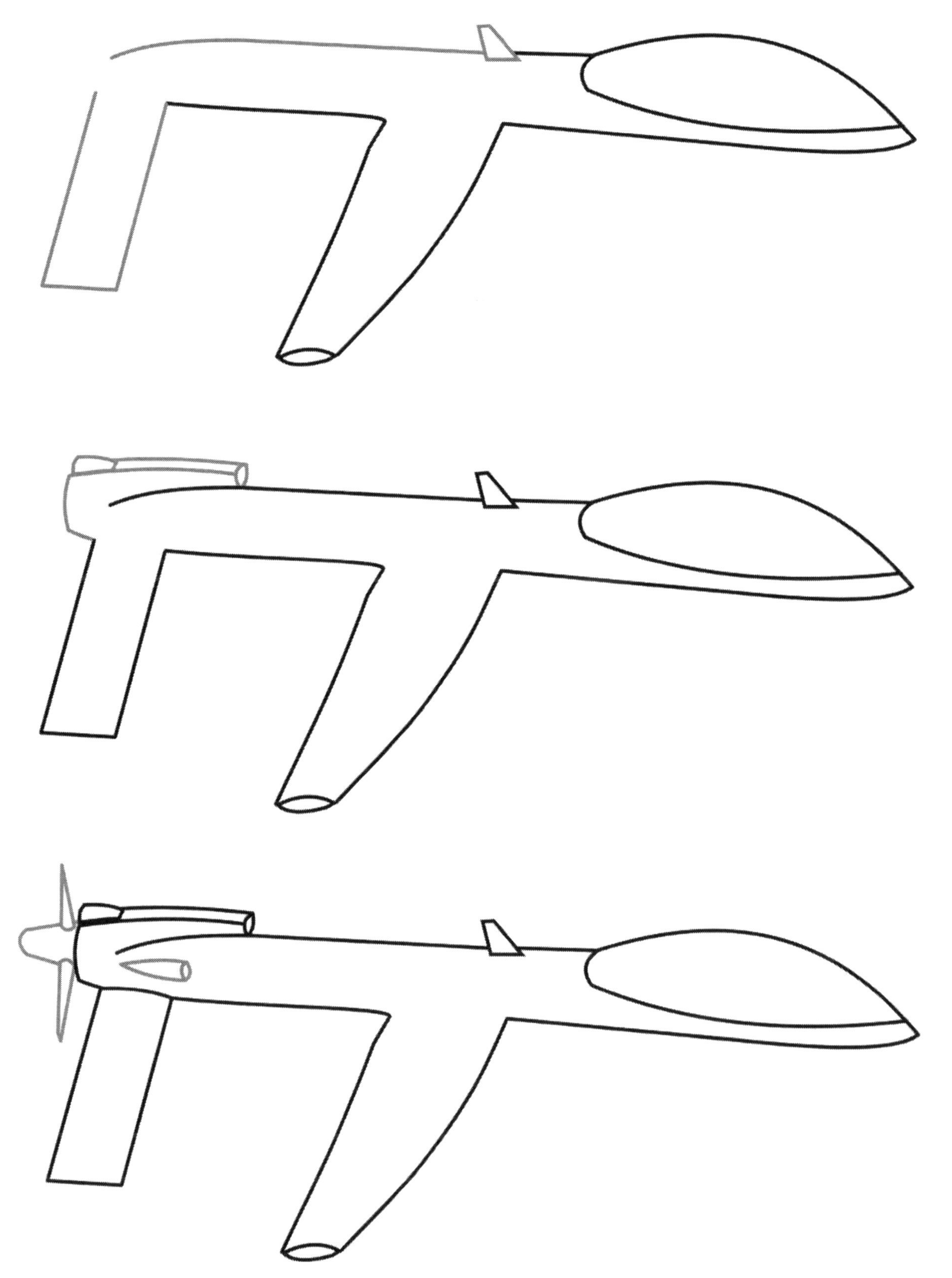

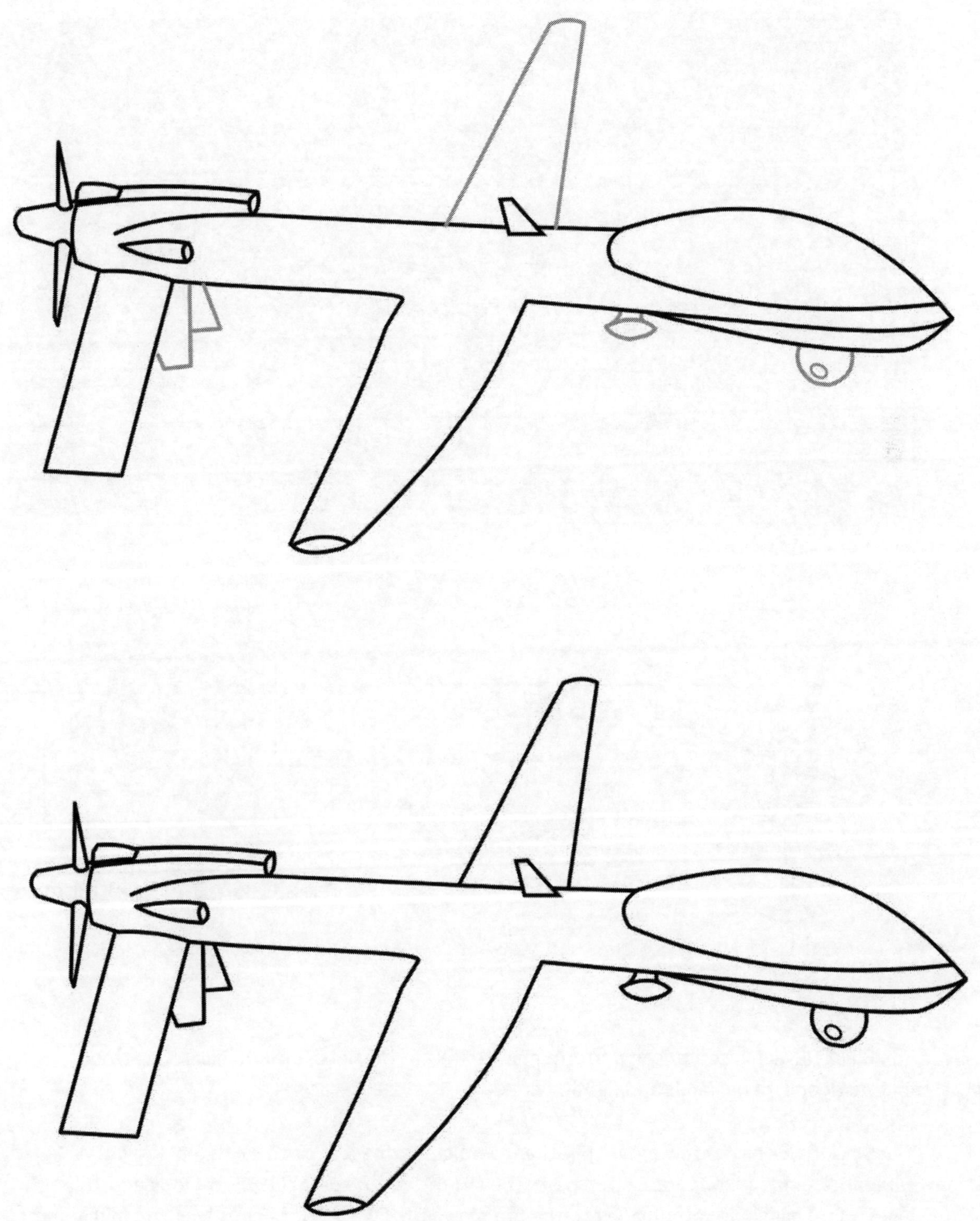

UH-60 BLACKHAWK

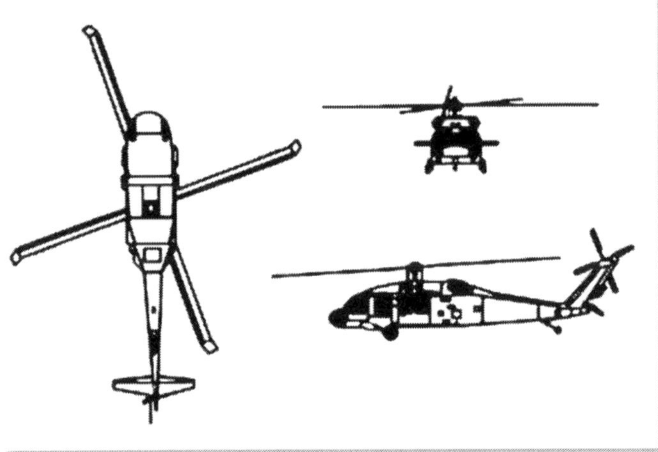

To see video of the UH-60 in action,
Click on the Quick Response (QR) code
above or visit
https://www.dvidshub.net/video/409747/blackhawk-ride#.VdIjYvlViko

The Black Hawk helicopter can perform many different missions, including carrying troops, flying injured people to hospitals and fighting fires.

The Black Hawk has a crew of two pilots and two crew chiefs. It can carry 2,640 lbs. (1,200 kg) of cargo including 11 troops or 6 stretchers. The UH-60 is 64 ft. 10 in. (19.76 m) long and 16 ft. 10 in. (5.13 m) high. The rotor blades on the top of the UH-60 are 53 ft. 8 in. (16.36 m) in diameter. Its top speed is 183 mph (294 km/h) and it can fly as high as 19,000 ft. (5,790 m).

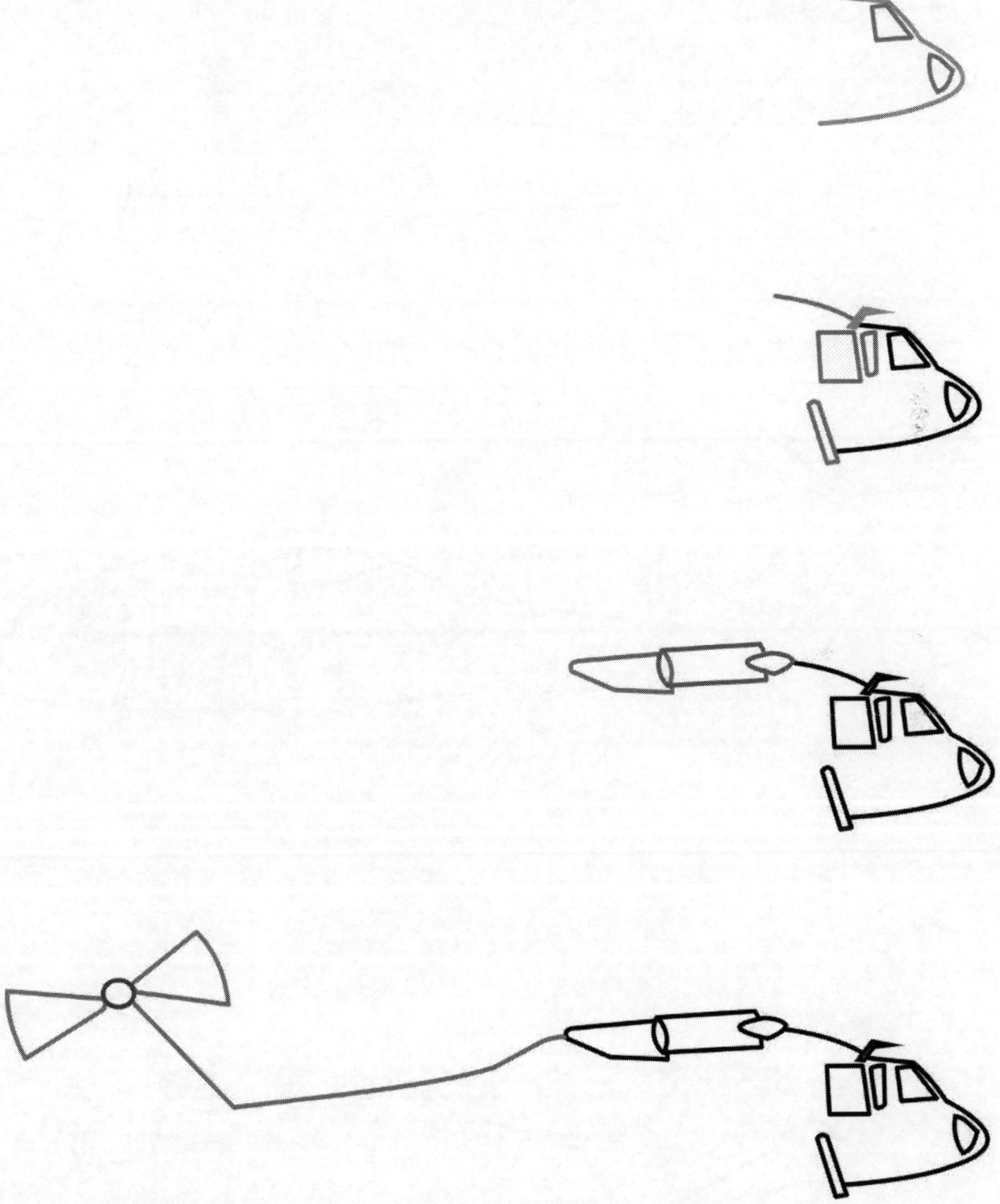

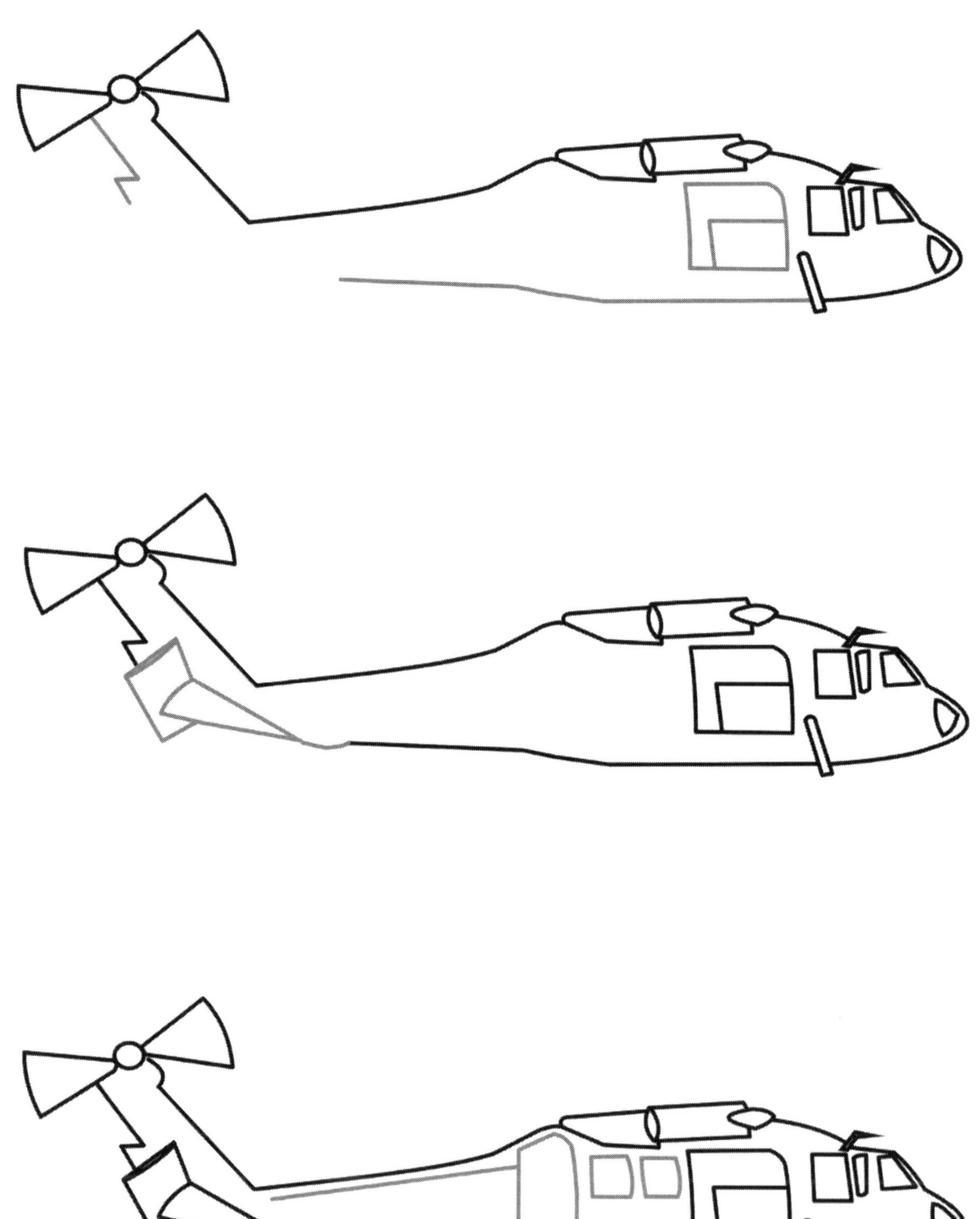

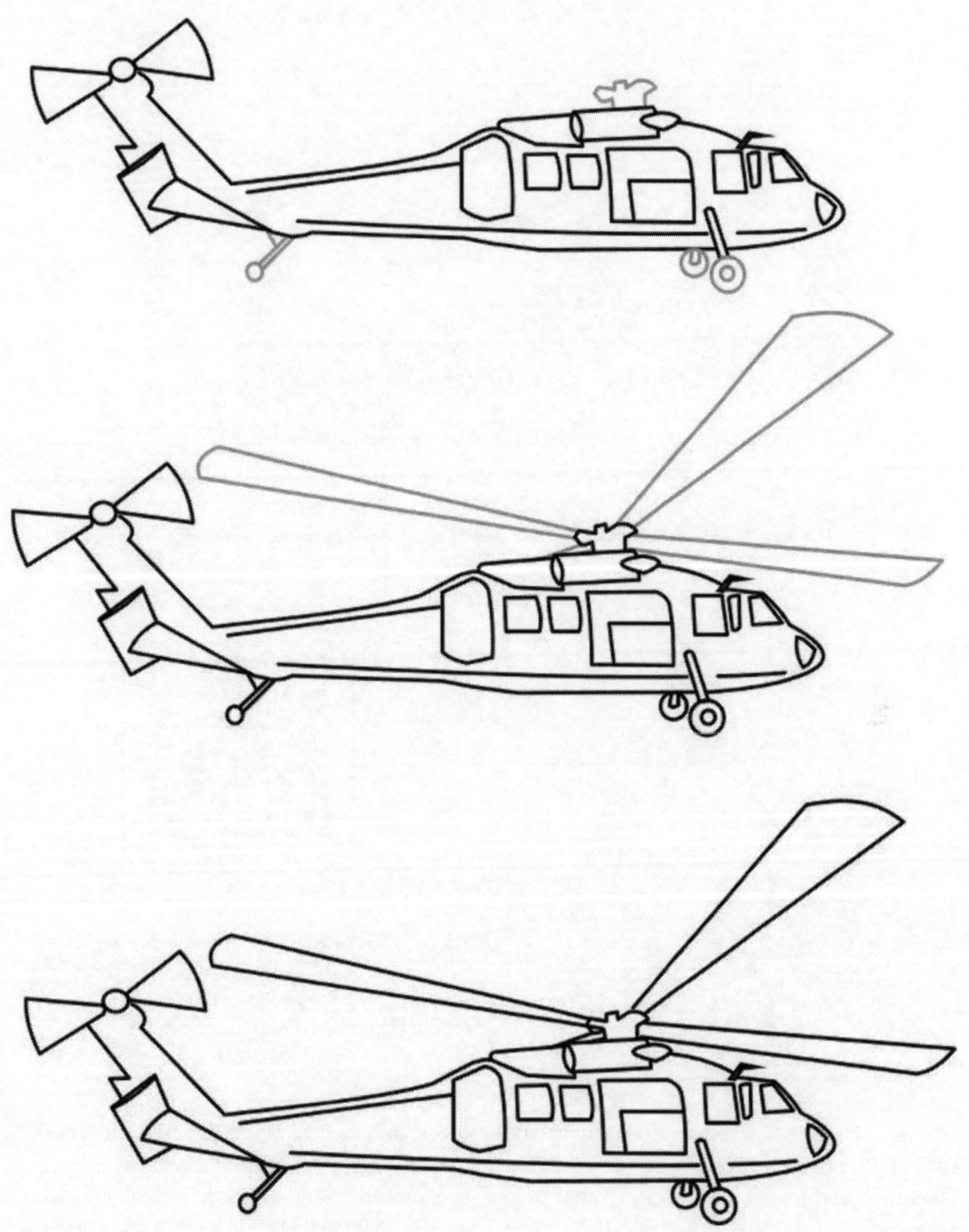

V-22 OSPREY

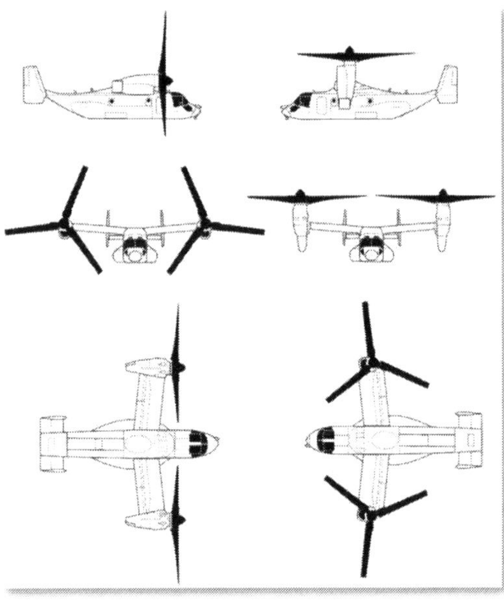

To see video of the V-22 in action,
Click on the Quick Response (QR) code
above or visit
https://www.youtube.com/watch?v=-KxZOGj1NJg

The V-22 Osprey is a tiltrotor aircraft that can take-off and land vertically like a helicopter. In about 12 seconds, the Osprey can turn its rotors down and fly like an airplane. In fact, the Osprey flies like an airplane about 75% of the time. The V-22 has a crew of four - a pilot, copilot and two flight engineers (also known as crew chiefs). The V-22 is 57 ft. 4 in. (17.5 m) long, 22 ft. 1 in. (6.73 m) high and it has a wing span of 45 ft. 10 in. (14 m). Its rotors have a diameter of 38 ft. (11.6 m) and it has a maximum speed of 316 mph (509 km/h). It can fly as high as 25,000 ft. (7,620 m).

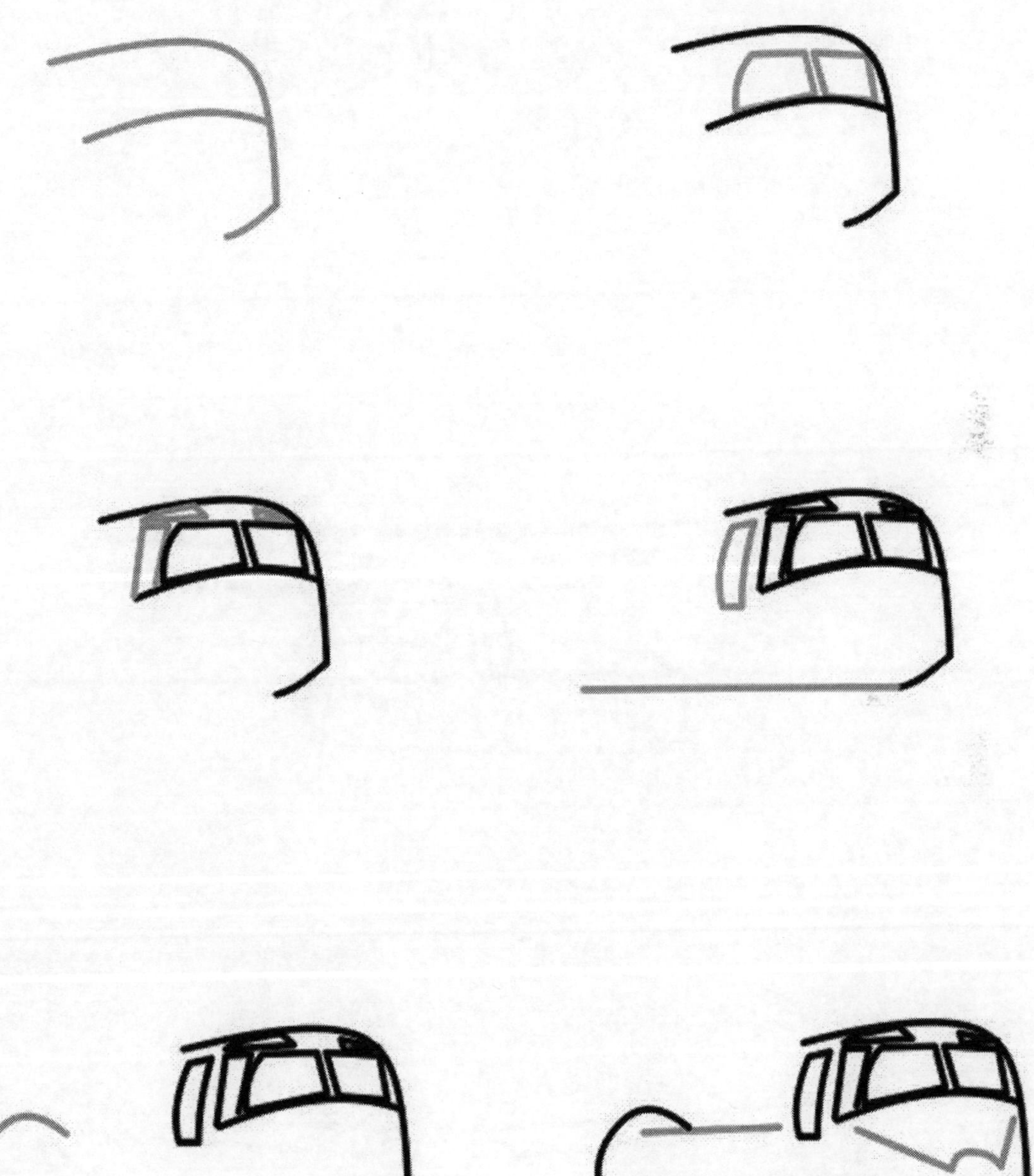

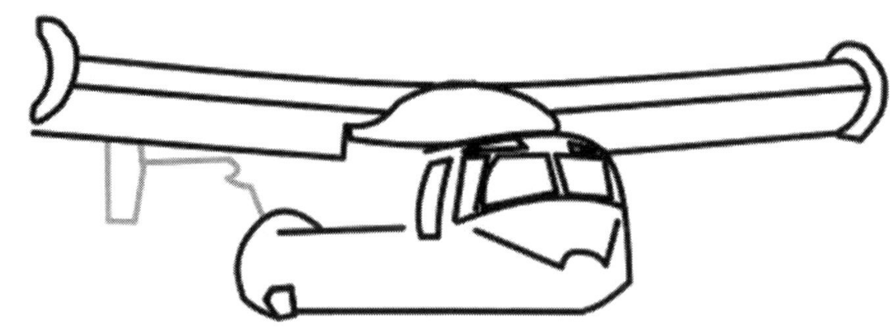

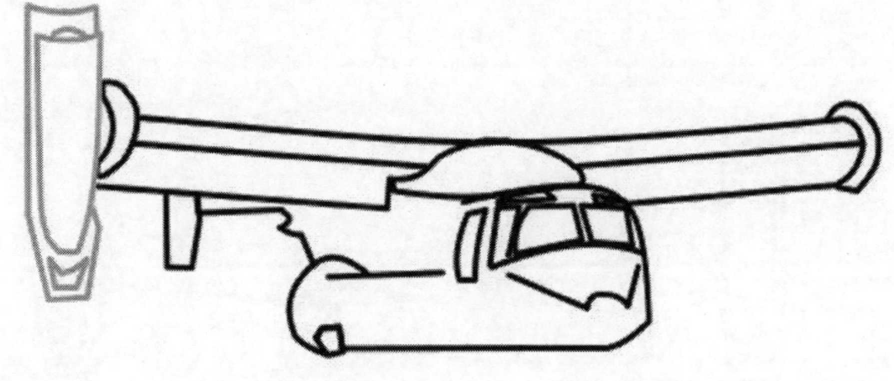

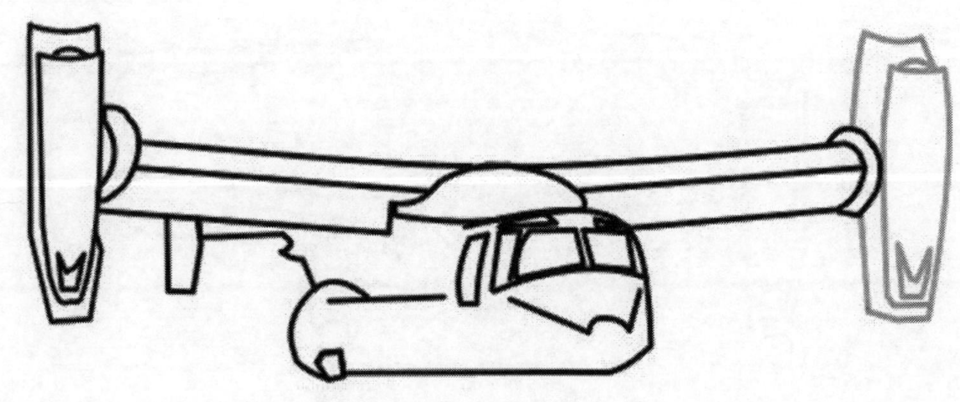

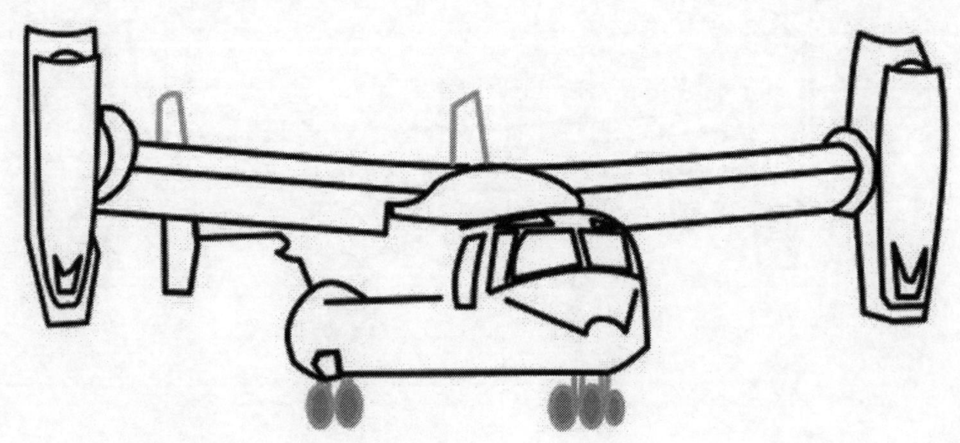

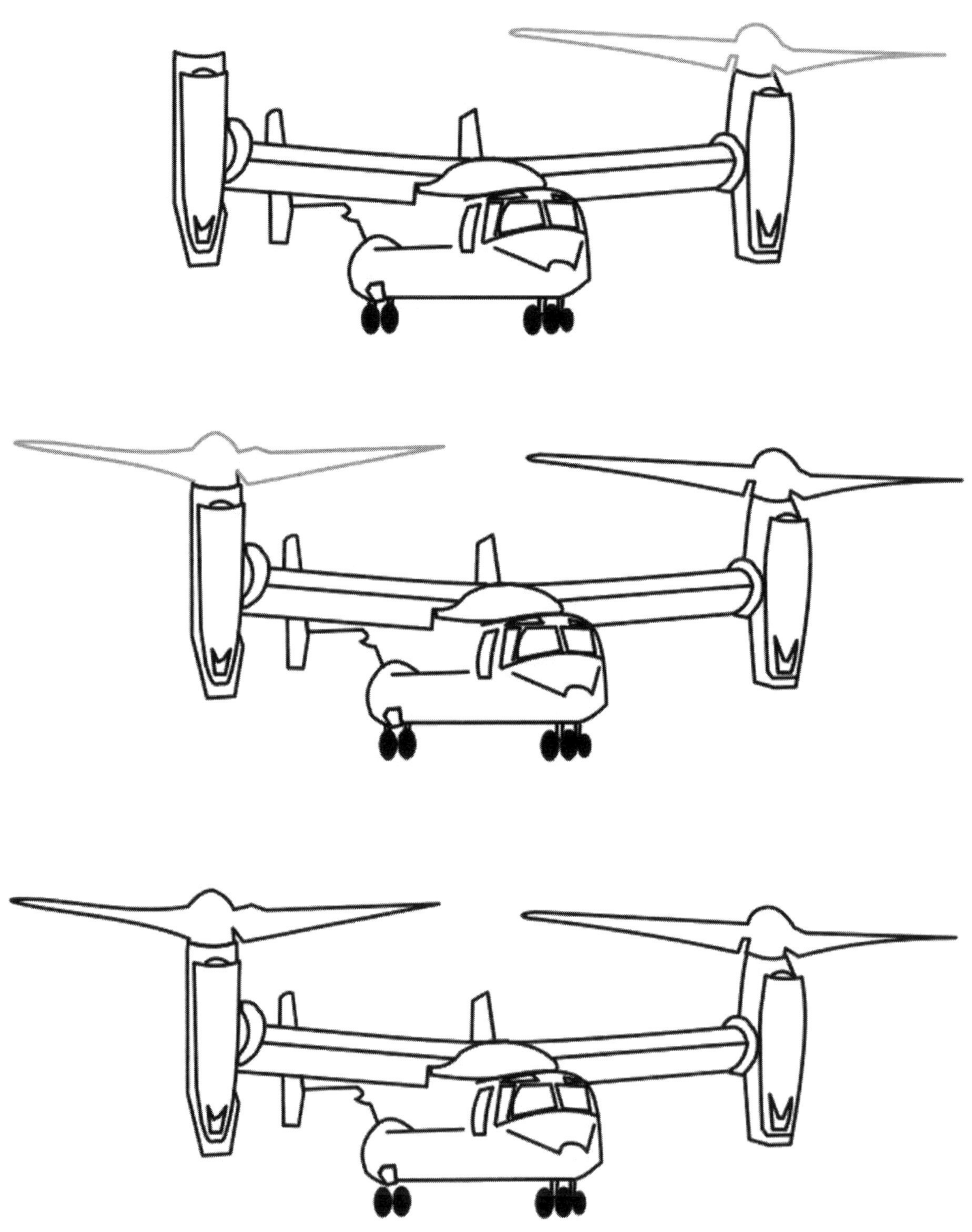

WANT MORE INFORMATION?

Your local public library or school library has lots of great information about jets, helicopters as well as other military aircraft. You can also find tons of information, pictures and videos about military aircraft on the Internet. Here are some kid-friendly web sites you might want to visit to learn more...

http://www.britannica.com/technology/military-aircraft
In addition to detailed information about military aircraft, this website has pictures, videos, quizzes and lists. Plus, you can learn about the history of flight from balloons to drones.

http://www.dkfindout.com/us/transportation/history-aircraft/
Learn about famous pilots and record-breaking aviation events. You can also learn about gliders, sport planes and other aircraft. Great pictures!

http://fas.org/man/dod-101/sys/ac/intro.htm
This web site is loaded with information about the parts of different aircraft, a detailed explanation of how aircraft fly, aviation terms and lots of illustrations. If you want to know the basics about aviation this is a great place to start.

http://www.nasa.gov/subject/7565/future-aircraft/
Get a peek into the future of aviation by visiting this NASA web site. Lots of experimental aircraft and amazing ideas for future designs. Pictures and videos!

http://mocomi.com/jet-planes/
Visit this website to watch a short video about important aircraft and dates in aviation history. Lots of "fun facts" too.

http://www.pbs.org/wgbh/nova/military/pilot-gear.html
This PBS web site has information about what pilots wear during flight and why each piece of the flight suit is important.

ABOUT THE AUTHOR/ILLUSTRATOR

Mike Artell has written and illustrated dozens of books. Mike's body of work includes books about outer space, weather, bugs and our sense of smell. He's also written and illustrated picture books, biographies, joke books, drawing books and professional books for teachers.

Mike regularly speaks at conferences and schools and conducts live webinars during which he shares his techniques for thinking, writing and drawing more creatively.

You can draw along with Mike on YouTube. Just do a search on, "Mike Artell." To learn more about Mike's books, videos and personal appearances visit www.mikeartell.com or click on the QR code below.